Islands of the Seals
The Pribilofs

Alaska Geographic®
Volume 9, Number 3

The Alaska Geographic Society

To teach many more to better know and use our natural resources

About This Issue: We've called upon a number of Aleut leaders, teachers, and those with special knowledge of the Pribilofs' natural resources to help compile this issue of *ALASKA GEOGRAPHIC®*. Craig A. Hansen put together an authoritative account of fur seals, and the historical and present-day state of sealing. Alton Y. and D. Colleen Roppel share their knowledge of the wild flowers which turn the Pribilof landscape into a patchwork of color in the summer. With tour guide experience in the Pribilofs, Elaine Rhode contributes her knowledge of the islands' physical environment and famed bird populations. We are grateful to C. Howard Baltzo and Regina and Bill Browne for sharing memories from their many years of residence on the Pribilofs, and to Larry Merculieff, born and raised on Saint Paul and now president of the Saint Paul village corporation, for his account of the traditional Aleut culture of the Pribilofs. Finally, Penny Rennick, Executive Editor, incorporates observations on the history and the future into this issue on the wildlife-rich, tradition-rich, Bering Sea outpost . . . the Pribilof Islands.

We appreciate the efforts of the many photographers who shared their material with us. And a special thanks goes to Daniel Gibson and R.H. Day for reviewing portions of the manuscript.

Chief Editor, Robert A. Henning
Assistant Chief Editor, Barbara Olds
Executive Editor, Penny Rennick
Editorial Assistant, Kathy Doogan
Designer, Ray Weisgerber   **Cartographer,** David Shott

ALASKA GEOGRAPHIC®, ISSN 0361-1353, is published quarterly by The Alaska Geographic Society, Anchorage, Alaska 99509-6057. Second-class postage paid in Edmonds, Washington 98020-3588. Printed in U.S.A. Copyright©1982 by The Alaska Geographic Society. All rights reserved. Registered trademark: Alaska Geographic. ISSN 0361-1353; Key title Alaska Geographic.

THE ALASKA GEOGRAPHIC SOCIETY is a nonprofit organization exploring new frontiers of knowledge across the lands of the polar rim, learning how other men and other countries live in their Norths, putting the geography book back in the classroom, exploring new methods of teaching and learning — sharing in the excitement of discovery in man's wonderful new world north of 51°16'.

MEMBERS OF THE SOCIETY RECEIVE *Alaska Geographic®*, a quality magazine which devotes each quarterly issue to monographic in-depth coverage of a northern geographic region or resource-oriented subject.

MEMBERSHIP DUES in The Alaska Geographic Society are $30 per year; $34 to non-U.S. addresses. (Eighty percent of each year's dues is for a one-year subscription to *Alaska Geographic®*.) Order from The Alaska Geographic Society, Box 4-EEE, Anchorage, Alaska 99509-6057; (907) 274-0521.

MATERIAL SOUGHT: The editors of *Alaska Geographic®* seek a wide variety of informative material on the lands north of 51°16' on geographic subjects — anything to do with resources and their uses (with heavy emphasis on quality color photography) — from Alaska, Northern Canada, Siberia, Japan — all geographic areas that have a relationship to Alaska in a physical or economic sense. We do not want material done in excessive scientific terminology. A query to the editors is suggested. Payments are made for all material upon publication.

CHANGE OF ADDRESS: The post office does not automatically forward *Alaska Geographic®* when you move. To insure continuous service, notify us six weeks before moving. Send us your new address and zip code (and moving date), your old address and zip code, and if possible send a mailing label from a copy of *Alaska Geographic®*. Send this information to *Alaska Geographic®* Mailing Offices, 130 Second Avenue South, Edmonds, Washington 98020-3588.

MAILING LISTS: We have begun making our members' names and addresses available to carefully screened publications and companies whose products and activities might be of interest to you. If you would prefer not to receive such mailings, please so advise us, and include your mailing label (or your name and address if label is not available).

Library of Congress cataloging in publication data:
Main entry under title:

Islands of the seals.
   (Alaska geographic, ISSN 0361-1353; v. 9, no. 3)
   1. Pribilof Islands (Alaska)—Description and travel.   2. Pribilof Islands (Alaska)—History.
3. Sealing—Alaska—Pribilof Islands.   I. Alaska Geographic Society.   II. Series.
F901.A266 vol. 9, no. 3 [F912.P9] 917.98s 82-8708
ISBN 0-88240-169-6   [979.8′4] AACR2

Cover—**Playing in the surf, these fur seals take to the water to keep cool and to escape any land-born disturbance.**
(Lael Morgan, Staff)

Previous page—**Fur seals from North Rookery cool off in the morning mist in this photo looking across North Anchorage to the village of Saint George.** (Douglas W. Veltre)

Perched on a small hill with the Bering Sea pounding at its door, the older section of the city of Saint Paul is home for the majority of the community's approximately 591 residents.
(Susan Hackley Johnson, reprinted from *ALASKA GEOGRAPHIC*®)

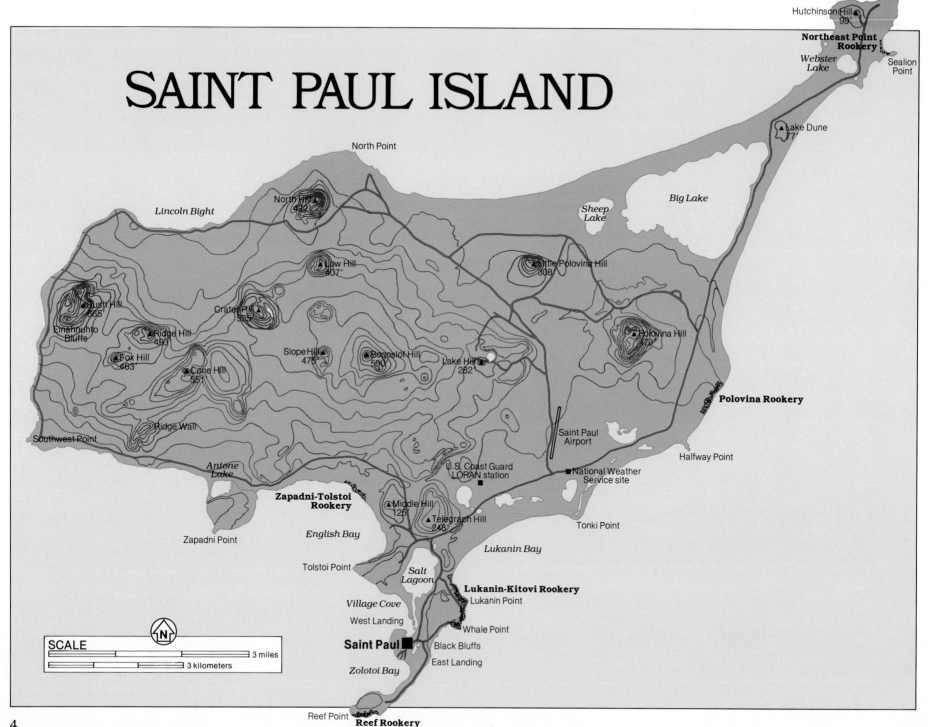

SAINT PAUL ISLAND

Northeast Point

Hutchinson Hill
99'

Northeast Point Rookery

Webster Lake

Sealion Point

▲Lake Dune
77'

North Point

Lincoln Bight

North Hill▲
432'

Sheep Lake

Big Lake

▲Low Hill
407'

▲Little Polovina Hill
308'

Rush Hill
665'

Crater Hill▲
535'

Einahnuhto Bluffs

▲Ridge Hill
493'

▲Polovina Hill
470'

▲Fox Hill
463'

Slope Hill▲
475'

Bogoslof Hill▲
590'

Lake Hill▲
282'

▲Cone Hill
551'

Polovina Rookery

Ridge Wall

Southwest Point

Saint Paul Airport

Halfway Point

Antone Lake

U.S. Coast Guard
LORAN station

■National Weather
Service site

Zapadni-Tolstoi Rookery

▲Middle Hill
125'

▲Telegraph Hill
248'

Tonki Point

Zapadni Point

English Bay

Lukanin Bay

Tolstoi Point

Salt Lagoon

Lukanin-Kitovi Rookery
Lukanin Point

Village Cove

West Landing

Whale Point

Saint Paul ■

Black Bluffs

Zolotoi Bay

East Landing

SCALE
N
3 miles
3 kilometers

Reef Point

Reef Rookery

Sea Lion Rock

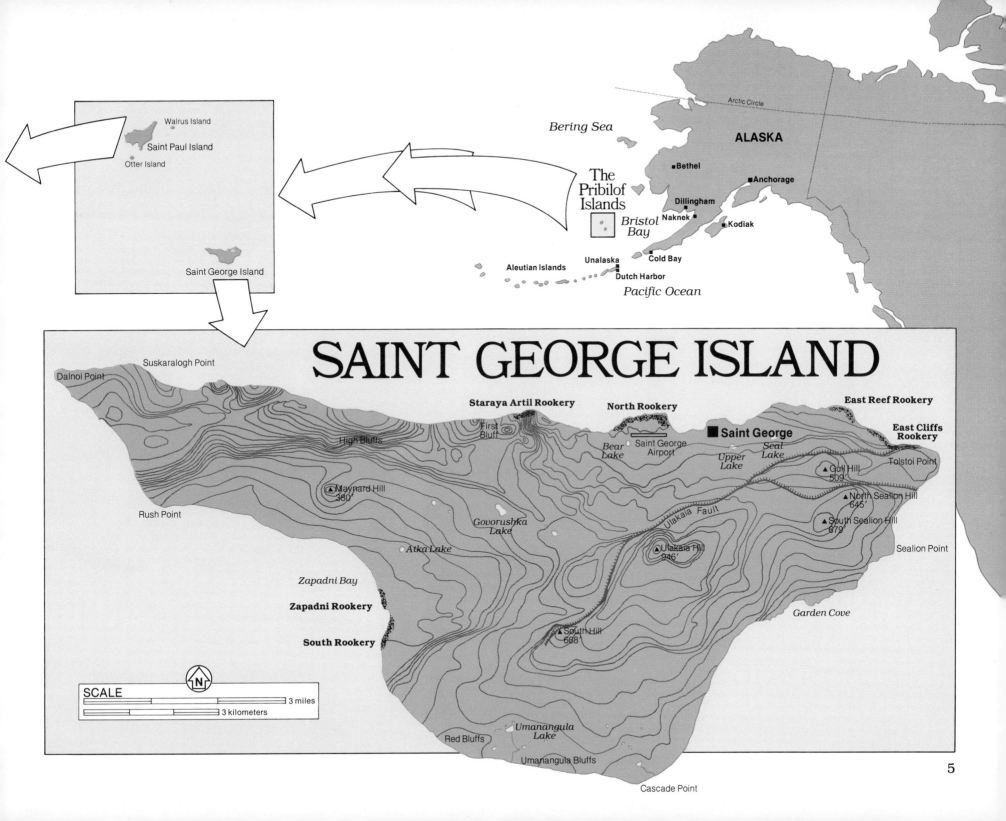

Walrus Island

Saint Paul Island

Otter Island

Saint George Island

Bering Sea

ALASKA

Arctic Circle

■Bethel

■Anchorage

The
Pribilof
Islands

■Dillingham

Naknek■

■Kodiak

*Bristol
Bay*

Unalaska

■Cold Bay

Aleutian Islands

Dutch Harbor

Pacific Ocean

SAINT GEORGE ISLAND

Suskaralogh Point

Dalnoi Point

Staraya Artil Rookery

North Rookery

East Reef Rookery

First
Bluff

■ **Saint George**

**East Cliffs
Rookery**

High Bluffs

*Bear
Lake*

Saint George
Airport

*Seal
Lake*

*Upper
Lake*

▲Gull Hill
509'

Tolstoi Point

▲Maynard Hill
380'

Rush Point

*Govorushka
Lake*

▲North Sealion Hill
645'

▲South Sealion Hill
679'

Atka Lake

Ulakala Fault

Sealion Point

▲Ulakaia Hill
946'

Zapadni Bay

Zapadni Rookery

Garden Cove

South Rookery

▲South Hill
668'

SCALE

Ⓝ

3 miles

3 kilometers

*Umanangula
Lake*

Red Bluffs

Umanangula Bluffs

Cascade Point

National Marine Fisheries Service

Introduction

There has been much written in recent years about the Aleuts and their way of life on the Pribilof Islands during the Russian years and until recently under America as times of "serfdom," "colonialism" and what many attorneys and activists have termed "slavery."

None of these terms are in a strict sense true. You will find some such terminology within this issue of *ALASKA GEOGRAPHIC®* composed of enough necessarily contemporary commentary to do a job of overview that jibes with these times. We do not wish to unnecessarily apply the editor's blue pencil, or to get into either philosophical or adversary discussions on the subject, but as a reporter and as a researching geographer for more years than most, we feel we must make a few declarations to plead for balance.

First, the term "serfdom" as it refers frequently to Aleuts of the Pribilofs under the Russians: One must remember that in the 18th and well into the 19th century, serfdom was both a part of the social structure and the economic *modus operandi* over much of the globe. It was not a Russian "mistreatment" of Aleuts far from the courts of the Czar . . . there was serfdom all over Russia . . . and in Great Britain . . . yes, and in early America. It was not "terrible" except in historical afterview.

As to the charges of "colonialism" and severe mandate control by various fur company managers and bureaucrats, following on a norm of generally accepted (quite probably even by the Aleuts in this instance) "serfdom," undoubtedly, as in all social structures there were sometimes managerial excesses. And in a long history of bureaucratic administration by various United States Government agencies, the Aleuts were not the only victims of bungling. Throughout Alaska, (and many other places in the world under other Government bureaucracies as well as American) there was first of all profound ignorance of geographic realities . . . government centers were far away and perhaps one might say the degree of stupidity in the fundamental geography of lands and people in question on the part of the Government increased in direct proportion to the distance between governed and those governing. The world itself was without efficient communication and with what today we know was then only the barest essentials of basic geographic knowledge . . . the better understanding that comes from better knowing climate, flora, fauna, economics, history, geology, sociology, even archaeology as well as anthropology. And today one must realize the Pribilofs are still considerable distance from "everything."

In Alaska's case, and in the case of the Pribilovians, as with other Natives, don't think too harshly of the years of stumbling management . . . neither administrators nor administered really knew then there was anything different. The important thing now (and this is the essence of why we created The Alaska Geographic Society) is that we better know these Pribilof Island resources . . . all of us . . . and thus better know each other and our place in swiftly moving time.

Robert A. Henning

President
The Alaska Geographic Society

Two elegant young ladies, Zsa Zsa Kochutin (left) and Jessica Rukovishnikoff, pose for photographers John and Margaret Ibbotson during a sunny day on Saint Paul.

9

A thin covering of snow glazes this January view of Saint Paul (population 591 according to a 1981 estimate), Village Cove lies just above the town, and Salt Lagoon just beyond. The National Marine Fisheries Service complex is to the right of Salt Lagoon.

Reeve Aleutian Airways provides passenger and freight service to Saint Paul with their Super Lockheed Electras. Planes land two or three times a week depending on the season and weather.

Islandscape

By Elaine Rhode

Flying 800 miles from Anchorage to the Pribilof Islands, one can be swept back 200 years to the deck of Gerassim Pribilov's ship, peering forever through dense fog, listening for the long-awaited bellow and bleat of fur seals. The decade of search for these misty isles with their treasure of furs is reenacted figuratively all too often as today's questing ships, the Super Lockheed Electras of Reeve Aleutian Airways, search for that hole in the clouds which reveals the destination.

The first island most visitors and returning villagers see is Saint Paul, largest of the five Pribilofs and equipped with a red cinder runway built during World War II. It is a rare treat to witness this island, less than 14 miles long and 8 miles wide, in its entirety on a blue sky and sunshine day.

If you are lucky, the multipeaked silhouette of Saint George Island lies almost as a mirage to the southeast of Saint Paul about 40 miles. Passengers, mail, and air cargo bound for that second largest of the Pribilofs are usually shuttled via Saint Paul in small aircraft from King Salmon or Cold Bay.

Editor's note: A former staff member of the U.S. Fish & Wildlife Service with several seasons' experience in the Aleutians, Elaine Rhode served as a tour guide on Saint Paul during the 1980 and 1981 summer tourist seasons.

Sitting on top of the
world, or at least on
top of Saint George,
a biologist surveys a
tundra and sea
landscape from the
roof of a seabird
colony at High
Bluffs. The village of
Saint George lies in
the distance.

B.E. Lawhead

Douglas W. Veltre

Sea urchins collect
in a tidepool on
Saint George. The
Pribilof people as
well as the islands'
immense wildlife
colonies rely on the
abundant and varied
marine life of the
Bering Sea for
sustenance.

A storm front moves in on three of the Pribilofs' five islands. Saint Paul with the catwalk for observing seals is in the foreground; Sea Lion Rock rises in the middle; Otter Island, seven miles south of Saint Paul, looms on the horizon.

Ric Robinson

13

Low, sandy beaches characterize Saint Paul and contrast sharply with the steep bluffs of Saint George.

Both photos by Douglas W. Veltre

Evidence of the islands' volcanic origins, lava nodules, smoothed by wave action close to the waterline but more jagged and angular higher up, are exposed under the tundra mat along Saint Paul's north shore.

The other three Pribilofs are inhabited only by the famed fur seals, seabirds, and sea lions and are seldom visited by humans. The black mound of Sea Lion Rock lies within a stone's throw of Reef Point, the southernmost tip of Saint Paul. Seals and cormorants occupy this islet. Otter Island rises like the prow of a three-quarter-mile-long ship to the south-southwest about five miles. Sea otters were hunted to extinction in this part of the Bering Sea before 1900. Walrus, too, no longer ply these waters or visit their island namesake about eight miles east of Saint Paul. Instead, Walrus Island hosts a crowd of sea lions along its third-of-a-mile length. The island is so low and narrow that storm seas wash over it, and thin sea fog often obscures its presence. Both Walrus and Otter islands are now incorporated in Alaska Maritime National Wildlife Refuge.

Fish-rich, shallow waters of the continental shelf surround the islands to a depth of about 330 feet. The shelf breaks and slopes to deeper oceanic water to the south and east. A recently charted, nutrient-laden current sweeps northeastward from the Pacific Ocean through the gap between the Aleutian and Commander islands and flows up the slope onto the continental shelf.

This current carries with it all the nitrates, phospates, silicates, and trace elements that support organisms at the bottom of the food chain, which in turn feed the incredible number of marine animals that give the Bering Sea a worldwide reputation. The fishing fleets off Pribilof shores, the fur seals on the beaches, and the seabirds on the cliffs are annual testimony to this richness.

Yet for all the surrounding aquatic wealth, the islands themselves are stark, a result of recent emergence from the sea. Geologists call the Pribilofs submarine hills and say they began forming 400,000 years ago, about the middle of the Ice Age. Volcanics compose most of the surface structure. Oozing from fissures in the ocean floor along two fault lines, basalts and other igneous rocks piled up gradually.

Cinder cones pushed up eventually, and several lava flows of jumbled, ragged rock remain as evidence to a once-active landscape. The Pribilofs are far enough north of the Aleutian arc to be out of the violent "Ring of Fire" that arches across the Pacific and continues to cause volcanic eruptions and frequent earthquakes. The Pribilof volcanoes are extinct, and tremors rarely shake Saint Paul or Saint George.

But the Bering Sea, pounding at the shorelines, tries to make up for that lack of earthly excitement. Stand on cliff tops during moderate storm seas, and

Penny Rennick, Staff

Randy Wiest lowers himself into a lava tube cave on Bogoslof, a 590-foot, twin-peaked cinder cone on Saint Paul.

B.E. Lawhead

The view looking west from the rim of High Bluffs shows some of the large seabird colonies for which the islands are famous. The bluffs rise more than 1,000 feet from Saint George's north shore.

you will feel the shock of each wave reverberate through the earth and rocks beneath your feet. Julie Melovidov of Saint Paul tells of sitting in a truck in winter atop the highest sea bluff on the island and being drenched by spray. Huge beach boulders tossed like pebbles create the natural sea walls for Salt Lagoon and Antone Lake on Saint Paul.

The battered coastline of Saint George soars skyward with the 2.5 million seabirds that nest there each summer. About 21 miles of rugged cliffs rise more than 200 feet, the highest reaching 1,012 feet at High Bluffs. Saint Paul, in contrast, is lower and more weathered with sand and rock beaches. Here sand dunes are more prevalent. Saint Paul has only seven miles of cliffs and only one and one-half miles of those top 200 feet, reducing potential seabird nesting habitat to one-eighth of Saint George's. Instead, the gradually sloping boulder

On Saint George a wooden cross marks the rocky trail over Ulakaia Ridge and across the island to Garden Cove. Travelers wedge coins into cracks in the wooden cross to ensure a safe journey.

Penny Rennick, Staff

16

B.E. Lawhead

Right—Luxuriant tundra entangles and topples many an unsuspecting hiker on the Pribilofs. Here a few stems of purple monkshood peak through a tangled mat of vegetation on Saint Paul.

Far right—The Pribilofs' entire population lives in two communities. About 158 people (1980 census) reside in Saint George, the smaller of the two communities and the only one on Saint George Island.

Both photos by Penny Rennick, Staff

interior. The slowly shifting dunes are pocked with blowouts caused by wind and slumping of the beach rye whose probing roots normally secure the sand. At Northeast Point shifting sand has joined what was once an islet to larger Saint Paul Island.

The islands' beaches, bluffs, and hills are named in a melody of Russian words — Lukanin, Ulakaia, Polovina, Marunich, Tolstoi, Dalnoi, Zapadni, Staraya Artil. Bogoslof, or "word of God," the 590-foot, twin-peaked cinder cone on Saint Paul, still bears the Russian cross erected on its summit in 1787 by the first recorded discoverers. On Saint George a wooden cross marks the rocky trail over Ulakaia Ridge and across the island to Garden Cove. Coins, placed there by travelers hoping for a safe journey, lie wedged into cracks in the weathered wood.

Each peak and high coastal bluff hold another reminder of earlier occupation: World War II observation dugouts. Arctic foxes and intrepid hikers are the only sentries these days.

Hikers to the interior of Saint Paul and Saint George must be intrepid because what looks like smooth approaches to the hills is deceptive. The tundra is gnarled in a mass of tussocks, gulleys, and slippery, grass-covered boulders, just waiting to topple unsuspecting hikers.

Movement near the coasts is made easier by about 27 miles of main road on Saint Paul and about 10 miles on Saint George. Nature handily supplied roadbed material in the form of scoria, or volcanic cinders, from the hillsides. Where winds fought roads across the sand dunes, remnants of planking, weathered silver with age, form the islands' closest thing to pavement — for all of 100 feet.

Only Saint George has a few short streams emptying into the sea. Except for three-mile-long Big Lake on Saint Paul, lakes on both islands are small and scattered. Some even lie in volcanic craters and are frequented by bathing kittiwakes and thirsty reindeer. Many are intermittent, relying on sufficient rainfall and runoff to become wet.

beaches so numerous on Saint Paul attract the majority of the Pribilof fur seals. Generations of lumbering bulls and scurrying pups have worn those black rocks smooth.

Sweeping black sand beaches fringe the eastern half of Saint Paul, and sand dunes creep toward the

Bill Browne

Craig A. Hansen

The islands are brown or white almost nine months of the year. Except in rare years of early springs, the rolling landscape shows its first spears of green at the beginning of June with the emerald lushness following hurriedly in recognition of the short growing season. The sites where year after year the Aleuts kill the fur seals turn green first and fastest so well fertilized are they. Den sites for artic foxes green early for the same reason — providing an easy way to spot them.

Typical Pribilof weather is fog, so thick that the world shrinks to a 500-foot radius. But atypical sunshine happens too. Then people flee the buildings to go for picnic drives, a beach walk, or three-wheeling around town.

The highest temperature recorded was 64° (August, 1936 and 1941). That may not seem hot, but local children are acclimated to swim at 55°F. Summer temperatures usually range from 37°F to 51°F. Typically there are only five days each winter when thermometers drop below the zero mark: the lowest on record is -26°F, but the usual range is from 19°F to 36°F.

Yearly precipitation totals about 24 inches. This includes from 22 to 139 inches of snow for an average of 59 inches. During the record winters of 1963-1964 and 1972-1973 when more than 100 inches of snow fell, villagers had to dig tunnels between houses.

Winds tend to make up for moderate temperatures in all seasons. Speeds have been clocked at 82 miles per hour, but 40 to 50 miles per hour are more typical in storms. Winds are a gentle 18 miles per hour average in summer with the first big blow of autumn hitting soon after mid-August.

With prolonged north and northeasterly winds in midwinter, the artic ice pack occasionally moves south to surround the islands with ice floes. Before air transportation, this meant months of isolation for the islands. Now Saint Paul's twice weekly and Saint George's twice monthly air service keeps the villages linked to the outside world regularly — weather permitting.

The Pribilofs' white coat is shed each summer to reveal a profusion of color sparkling in the lush tundra.

Whitish gentian grow in patches among fields of lupines near the Saint Paul airstrip. Sometimes the flower is white, sometimes bluish-purple.

With vigor renewed by a long period of winter dormancy and encouraged by rising air temperatures of spring, the flowering plants of the Pribilof Islands almost overnight transform seemingly endless desolation and the grayish-brown remains of the twilight months into the luxuriant growth of summer. The Pribilofs are no different from any other region in the world where vegetation covers and protects the land in that variations in elevation, moisture content and type of soil, and mean air temperature combine to significantly affect plant growth and to a large extent determine species location. Rolling hills, numerous cinder cones, and vast areas of sand typical of Saint Paul Island contrast sharply with geologically younger Saint George Island, much of which consists of a landscape strewn with moss- and lichen-covered boulder fields. Even so, but in varying degrees of abundance, these two major islands within the Pribilof group are essentially host to the same species of flowering plants, most of which occur elsewhere in Alaska as well.

Foggy and at best, overcast skies, are the general rule for the Bering Sea region in June, July, and August, the months during which the flowering plants are at their best. An extremely humid

A Bouquet of Blossoms
By Alton Y. and D. Colleen Roppel

Editor's note: Alton Roppel, a wildlife research biologist with the National Marine Fisheries Service for 32 years, spent more than 25 years studying the fur seal herd of the Pribilof Islands. Joined by his wife Colleen during several summers of field research on the Pribilofs, both became interested in the wild flowers there and in 1980 photographed and collected some 100 of Saint Paul Island's more conspicous species.

The view to the east from the interior of Otter Island sweeps across tundra and fields of arctic poppies.

Craig A. Hansen

another does in fact occur; however, very definite and distinctly different habitats become evident as one takes the time to look about.

We find first of all that the taller varieties tend to flourish in lowland areas whereas higher elevations support vegetation scarcely three to four inches in height. As we fly over Big and Sheep lakes and swing around and behind Polovina Crater and onto a mile-long landing strip located in the eastern flatland of Saint Paul Island, we see vast fields of color dominated by the blue of lupine *(Lupinus nootkatensis)* accented here and there with a few stalks of its creamy-white color phase. In places where this species thins and loses its influence over the growth of others, stately monkshood *(Aconitum delphinifolium)* springs to life as do isolated clumps of nodding lychnis *(Lychnis apetala)* and patches of whitish gentian *(Gentiana algida)* with flowers of bluish-purple and white in various combinations of dominance. Here also is where ground-hugging crowberry *(Empetrum nigrum),* much used by the Aleuts in making pies and jelly, is most abundant. A few Aleuts still attach the odoriferous root of the herb valerian *(Valeriana capitata),* called *ahmin* locally, to their halibut bait to increase its attraction to the fish.

To the north and east, the area surrounding the airport eventually gives way to a quarter-mile-wide strip of sand interrupted along its 16-mile length only by Polovina and Northeast Point rookeries. It is along this strip that beach rye grass *(Elymus arenarius)* has taken hold over the years and eventually subdued the effects of ever-shifting winds as they shaped and molded thousands upon thousands of cubic yards of sand. In dunelike areas, pockmarked with blowouts down to old beach rocks, lie bleached remains of several species of marine mammals such as walrus, northern or Steller sea lion, and whales of one kind or another. This area also supports such sand-loving species as the showy seabeach ragwort *(Senecio pseudo-arnica)* with its shiny leaves and multiple flowers. At the opposite end of the scale in terms of size is

environment and a daily dose in summer of nearly 20 hours of daylight quickly stimulate plant life into photosynthesis, the means by which flora everywhere use energy from the sun to manufacture chlorophyll and combine and convert carbon dioxide, water, and inorganic salts into growth and the seeds of reproduction. The floral community is actually made up of several parts; within each certain species have adapted for survival within a given environment. There are really no totally distinct boundaries, for considerable overlapping of some species of flowering plants from one part to

Far left—**Pribilof residents value the crowberry as an important ingredient for pies and jellies.**

Left—**Bulbous flowers of lupines, usually blue but occasionally creamy-white, dominate large patches of Saint Paul's landscape.**

Far left—**Last reported blooming on Saint Paul in 1885, the coastal fleabane or pink daisy was rediscovered by the authors when they came upon a single clump growing at Whitney Pond.**

Left—**The chocolate lily, more abundant on Saint George than Saint Paul, has striking deep purple flowers and edible roots.**

All photos by Alton Y. and D. Colleen Roppel

25

Bright flowers of the arctic poppy line some roadsides on Saint Paul.

second contract with the federal government to harvest the fur seals), the lunarlike moonwort *(Botrychium lunaria)* emerges from sandy soil to the right of the road. And almost everywhere, it seems, we find the seacoast angelica *(Angelica lucida)*, locally called *puuchkii*. Adults and children consume the plant's celerylike stalks.

Moving to the southwestern part of Saint Paul Island, we walk among volcanic rock jutting from the soil which, when combined with swirling fog-laden air, creates a moorlike atmosphere. Here may be found the primrose *(Primula tschuktschorum)* in all its pinkish splendor, but only very early in the season for by June's end the primrose has already shed its flowers and gone to seed. This species is eventually replaced by the arctic daisy *(Chrysanthemum arcticum)* throughout the remaining summer months as the most conspicuous species in the area. The hairy cinquefoil *(Potentilla villosa)* is also fairly abundant here, finding root not only in the ground but up through and into cracks and crevices in the volcanic rock. Nearby may be seen several clumps of beautiful moss campion *(Silene acaulis)*. And scattered here and there are patches of reindeer lichen *(Cladonia* sp.), a species sought by several hundred of these animals living on Saint Paul Island and a few animals living on Saint George.

In contrast to lowland areas, the Bering Sea water carpet *(Chrysosplenium wrightii)* survives only in scoria streaks on wind-swept slopes of once-active cinder cones such as North Hill. Between such streaks, the netleaf willow *(Salix reticulata)* acts to anchor the soil in place as its trunk and limbs creep ever so slowly along the ground in the process of growing taller through the years. On relatively level land below, the starflower *(Trientalis europaea)* springs forth from beds of moss. Also in the interior, but in entirely different settings, the diminutive snow primrose *(Primula nivalis)* thrives among rocks at water's edge along the western shore of Kittiwake Pond. Here too may be seen sibbaldia *(Sibbaldia procumbens)* along

the minute and extremely inconspicuous slender or delicate gentian *(Gentiana tenella)*. Blue in color, it stands scarcely two inches high at the most and is easily overlooked in the land between Polovina Bridge and the sea. Just beyond the plank road on the approach to Northeast Point, the delicate alkali buttercup *(Ranunculus cymbalaria)* enjoys dark moist sand over which it sends stolons, or runners, along which new plants spring to life. Further on, almost to the Webster House (Daniel Webster was an official of the Northern Commercial Company in the 1800s, a San Francisco-based firm that held the

Alton Y. and D. Colleen Roppel

Alton Y. and D. Colleen Roppel

Douglas W. Veltre

Alton Y. and D. Colleen Roppel

Far left—Sand dunes and beaches on Saint Paul provide suitable habitat for the seabeach ragwort.

Left—Only scoria streaks on wind-swept slopes of cinder cones support Bering Sea water carpet (*Chrysosplenium wrightii*).

Far left—Cloudberries or salmonberries add to the Pribilof people's subsistence food stock.

Left—The seacoast angelica or *puuchkii* has a tender stalk which the Aleuts consider a tasty morsel. Some Native cultures use the plant as a medicinal remedy.

27

The fleshy moonwort, shown here on Saint Paul Island, grows in woods, muskegs, open slopes, and meadows throughout most of Alaska south of the Brooks Range and is widely distributed through Canada, Europe, and Asia.

Alton Y. and D. Colleen Roppel

the eastern shore, distinctive not for its flowers but for its three-pointed leaves. The Siberian aster *(Aster sibiricus)* bursts into brilliant and almost irridescent color at the western base of Telegraph Hill as well as along the crest of a low ridge above Ice House Lake, from which the village people once drew their household water and cut blocks of ice in winter for use the following summer. On the flanks of Telegraph Hill and elsewhere grows northern wormwood *(Artemisia tilesii)*, a plant used locally to swathe affected joints and diminish the pain of arthritis.

Just below, alpine bistort *(Polygonum viviparum)* and marsh cinquefoil *(Potentilla palustris)* grow tall within the boggy confines of Ice

Bones of this female fin or finback whale, which washed up on Saint Paul's north shore, will eventually become enmeshed in the tangled mass of tundra that blankets much of the Pribilofs.

Douglas W. Veltre

House Lake itself. In an even more watery environment, such moisture-loving plants as rush form clumps at the margins of several of the fresh-water ponds and lakes found on the island. And in one of these ponds just across the road that winds along Salt Lagoon and in still another at the eastern base of Ridge Wall, mare's tail *(Hippuris vulgaris)* seeks sustenance in mud covered with a half-foot of water. The wild geranium *(Geranium erianthum)* grows only at Whitney Pond between Ridge Wall and the sea, just as does a single clump of coastal fleabane or pink daisy *(Erigeron peregrinus)*. So far as we know, we were the first to rediscover the latter species following a 95-year absence from view. It was last reported blooming on Saint Paul Island in 1885.

Cloudberry *(Rubus chamaemorus)*, which Aleuts also use in making jelly, grows in yet another environment, *Kaminista* or rocky place. Here too is the only place on Saint Paul where we found the chocolate lily *(Fritillaria camschatcensis)*. Numbering only a handful of plants here but abundant on Saint George, the lily's purplish flowers and edible rice roots are difficult to find amid dense growths of tall Jacob's ladder *(Polemonium acutiflorum)* and willow herb *(Epilobium behringianum)*. And nearby is a former lake bed that now supports a large field of russet cotton grass *(Eriophorum russeolum)*.

We could continue in an attempt to coax others away from the easily accessible roadside arctic poppy *(Papaver radicatum)*, which seems to prefer disturbed areas such as these, and into the interior of the island where the intrepid explorer can descend into small and relatively shallow inland craters. In just such sunken places as these snow persists late in the year, summer is delayed into autumn, and earlier blooming species more tolerant of extremes in elevation can be found much later than normal. The elegant sudetan lousewort *(Pedicularis sudetica)* is one of these species, just as is the rusty saxifrage *(Saxifraga hieracifolia)*.

The netleaf willow anchors the soil in place as its trunk and limbs creep along the ground as the tree ages.

28

Penny Rennick, Staff

A pair of adult red-legged kittiwakes greet one another, while just below them an adult keeps a close watch on its youngster. About 222,300 of this species live on Saint George.

Douglas W. Veltre

Tourists scan the bird rookeries at Ridge Wall, while murres line the first ledge below the tundra on the right.

For those who appreciate birds, traveling to the Pribilofs is like traveling to Mecca.

- Number one seabird colony in Alaska for abundance, diversity, and importance of species.
- One of the largest seabird colonies in the Northern Hemisphere.
- Main stronghold for the rare red-legged kittiwake, which breeds only in the Pribilofs, two Aleutian islands, and Russia's Commander Islands.
- One of the largest (1.5 million) colonies of thick-billed murres in the Bering Sea, if not the world.

All this occurs under seemingly inhospitable conditions: fog or mist, temperatures from about 40°F to 50°F, and buffeting winds averaging 18 miles per hour.

Some of those winds are favorable for bringing other birds, rare international migrants, to the islands as well: Mongolian plovers, Oriental cuckoos, Polynesian tattlers, Siberian rubythroats. To date 194 species have been spotted at least once since 1840 when Bishop Veniaminov published the first list of about a dozen birds.

From Masses to Migrants
The Story of the Pribilof Birds
By Elaine Rhode

31

R.H. Day

B.E. Lawhead

Above—**Among the rarest of North America's seabirds, the red-legged kittiwake breeds only in the Pribilofs, two Aleutian Islands, and Russia's Commander Islands.**

Above right—**The Pribilofs support the Bering Sea's largest colony of thick-billed murres. These diving seabirds sometimes reach depths of 240 feet in their search for small fish, their chief prey.**

calmly on a ledge in the daylight after their shift tending their egg in a dark crevice chamber.

The air buoys soaring northern fulmars, circling the cliffs many times before landing by their mates or flying out to sea to feed. Cormorants, like long-necked geese, pump by on black wings with fishy meals for their two to four always-hungry, naked chicks. Below in the surf, rafts of harlequin ducks paddle on the swells and dive under cresting waves. Beyond the breakers lines of off-duty murres and auklets bathe and socialize.

In the sparse upland tundra, rock sandpipers sit camouflaged on a cup nest or semipalmated plovers run in distraction displays while their chicks, speckled puffs on long legs, freeze in hiding. Winter wrens, more abundant on Saint George than Saint Paul, flit from one umbel to the next.

Lapland longspurs glide to earth on set wings, warbling their love symphony. Gray-crowned rosy finches dart in and out of old buildings or from cliff faces as they bring food to the second nest of chicks of the season. White and black snow buntings flit from one rock outcrop to the next, singing their territorial boundary.

Oldsquaws, heads bobbing in courtship, swim on one of the ponds or the lagoon. A flock of pintail

Below left—**Another member of the Pribilof alcid — seabirds that breed on shore, nest in colonies, and lay one or two eggs — community is the crested auklet, much darker than the smaller least or slightly larger parakeet auklets.**

Below—**A red-faced cormorant peers from its rocky perch on Saint Paul. In breeding season these birds have a bright red face patch and blue throat.**

New birds are still being added. Chimney swift, little stint, and curlew sandpiper were the most recent discoveries. Sometimes birds new to the Pribilofs are also the first records of such birds appearing in North America. In the 1960s William Sladen, Max Thompson, and Robert DeLong added nine birds to this continent's roll call through observations on the Pribilofs.

People have come from Germany, Switzerland, Africa, Australia, New Zealand, Venezuela, Britain, and Japan as well as Canada and all the United States to witness the phenomenon of birds.

What do they see? Cliff faces alive with growling murres and raucously squawking kittiwakes perched on narrow ledges or flying in to relieve mates at the nest. Horned and tufted puffins squeezing from cracks in the cliff face where they lay their single egg. Least and crested auklets jostling for perches while parakeet auklets sit

Craig A. Hansen

Douglas W. Veltre

Douglas W. Veltre

John and Margaret Ibbotson

John and Margaret Ibbotson

John and Margaret Ibbotson

Top far left—**An elegant gray-crowned rosy finch, one of nearly 200 species of birds recorded for the Pribilofs, rests briefly on a lichen-covered rock on the Saint George uplands.**

Top left—**Taking advantage of a rare moment of summer sunshine, a parakeet auklet (left) and least auklet resemble bowling pins slightly out of kilter. Parakeets average about 10 inches, while least auklets, smallest of the Pribilof auklets, reach about seven inches.**

Bottom far left and left—**Large, brightly colored bills identify puffins, perhaps the most colorful and popular of the Pribilofs' seabird residents. A white belly and absence of tufts distinguish the horned (left) from the tufted puffin (right).**

drakes takes off from a lake while on the fringes in the tall grasses a pintail hen squats over her brood of ducklings. A male northern phalarope dive-bombs an intruder too close to his chicks, his sole responsibility since the flashier female laid the eggs and left.

Shorebirds, waterfowl, and songbirds are in uncounted abundance. Pelagic or ocean-living birds have been studied for several years because of potential offshore oil leasing nearby in the Saint George Basin of the outer continental shelf. Pelagics have been estimated to number 2.8 million here, 2.5 million of those flocking to the cliffs and talus boulders of Saint George Island.

What attracts and sustains such great populations is the food-rich waters of the Bering Sea, especially the shallower continental shelf waters that surround the islands. Not only do the birds that nest on these Alaska islands utilize fish and crustaceans of the Bering Sea, but an estimated 9 to

33

R.H. Day

R.H. Day

Above—**A winter wren, common on Saint George but rare on Saint Paul, perches on the umbel of a** *puuchkii.* **Scientists are uncertain why the wrens are abundant on one island and not on the other, but speculate that they prefer cliff habitat which is more common on Saint George.**

Above middle—**The only member of the shearwater, petrel, and fulmar family to breed in Alaska, northern fulmars (light and dark phases shown here) resemble gulls but have tubular nostrils and longer, more slender wings.**

10 million short-tailed shearwaters retreating from winter in the Southern Hemisphere may become the most abundant species June through September. Just west of Otter Island in August of 1981 a mass of shearwaters was seen that extended more than two miles and was so densely black that at first glance it looked like a new island.

Competition among species is lessened both by feeding methods and by food preferences. Some birds, such as northern fulmars, forage about 65 miles offshore; others like the cormorants fish within two or three miles of the colonies. Thick-billed murres, which feed in the same areas as do the fulmars, seek their fish by diving, sometimes to depths of 240 feet, while the fulmars are surface or near-surface feeders.

Least and crested auklets and horned puffins all feed within a few miles of their colonies and by diving, but they choose different size prey or different species. Thus the Bering banquet table serves them all.

Mark Rauzon

Soammes Summerhays (left) from England, Francois Gohier (center) from France, and Francisco Erize from Argentina are just three of the thousands of tourists from around the world that come to view the Pribilofs' wildlife colonies.

Coexistence continues as birds sort themselves on the crowded cliffs. Each species has slightly varying maternity ward requirements.

Cormorants, first to build nests and lay eggs — usually in early May — choose ledges broad enough to hold a single, bulky pile of grass and seaweed. Murres nest later, in early to mid-June, and choose broad ledges too but seem to prefer ones big enough to accommodate many pairs. Ornithologists say crowding triggers their breeding cycle. Murres do not bother to make a nest but rather lay their turquoise eggs on bare rock, incubating them between belly and feet and each passing their single egg to their mate's feet at shift time. That is why disturbance —especially by low-flying aircraft or other loud noises — causes a rain of eggs as murres take flight in fright.

The two types of murres, common and thick-billed, further segregate themselves in nest sites by the width of the ledges: common murres gather on wider ones.

The two kittiwakes differentiate by elevation: black-legged kittiwakes prefer small ledges on lower sections of cliffs, rarely above 600 feet; red-legged kittiwakes choose overhung ledges beneath black-legs or the highest cliff faces. Thus Saint George, with nine miles of cliffs more than 400 feet

A raft of murres swim quietly on the waters below Ridge Wall.

Douglas W. Veltre

Egg gatherers descend a steep slope on Saint George looking for murre eggs. Murres usually will re-lay an egg lost to storm or accident or predation, but a chick born late in the season may not survive autumn storms.

Both photos by Douglas W. Veltre

This long bamboo pole with pincers at one end is used to grasp eggs from sea cliff nests.

high and one-third of those surpassing 600 feet, attracts and accommodates most of the red-legged kittiwakes — about 222,800. Saint Paul's shorter cliffs, none of which rises more than 400 feet, host an estimated 2,800.

In general, all pelagic birds are more abundant on Saint George than Saint Paul because the smaller island's cliff face area is eight times greater.

Least auklets on both main islands, however, prefer beach boulders and talus rubble over cliff crevices as home sites. Ulakaia Ridge, a stark, almost mile-long boulder talus inland from the village of Saint George, awakens each April even before snows melt when the least auklets come to court. As the season progresses, until the chicks fledge in early August, the swift-flying least auklets become familiar sights careening inland in morning and evening rush hours along a slight ridge between the village and the airstrip.

On Saint Paul their smokelike swarms can be seen over the barrier beaches of East Landing, Salt Lagoon, and Antone Lake. The auklets circle and dip over their colonies before landing or going to sea to feed.

A typical sight on the boulder beaches and cliff faces is a prowling arctic fox. In fact, foxes often make their den sites among the seabirds on the cliffs. Nimble as cats and about the same size, these brazen predators can maneuver on the tiniest

foothold to reach eggs, young, and sometimes even adult birds. Their well-used trails along cliff tops become littered with murre eggs that they brought up from below. Carcasses, usually only wings remaining, mark dens. Some ornithologists are worried that the high fox population, lately untrapped, is depleting the Pribilof bird resource.

Certainly, without fox predation the birds would spread their nest areas to grassy bluffs and cliff tops and more exposed ledges. Most birds were pushed to the sheer cliff faces or deepest crevices as an adaptation to the presence of the foxes. Open slope nesters such as glaucous-winged gulls were simply eliminated from the main islands after the first foxes stepped from ice floes that link the Pribilofs to the mainland in winter.

The local villagers still take advantage of the bird cliffs as a seasonal grocery store. It is traditional, especially on Saint George, to eat the red-legged kittiwake each spring before they nest. On Saint Paul they are more often shot in the fall.

Egging is another tradition for Pribilovians. Egg gatherers seek the freshly laid eggs of the murres, usually making a party of the occasion if the weather is nice in June. The bolder hunters dangle along the cliffs on ropes. Others use long poles with two flexible strips lashed to the end to act as

Left—The Pribilofs' seabird colonies stand out as some of the largest and most diverse in the Northern Hemisphere. By far the largest number of seabirds; such as the northern fulmars, red-legged kittiwakes, and thick-billed murres shown here; breed on Saint George where steep bluffs provide nesting ledges and safety from predators.

Above—Keeping an eye out in all directions, a cluster of parakeet auklets rests on a rocky ledge on one of the famed Pribilof fur seal rookeries.

Both photos by R.H. Day

pincers. They gather several dozen to several hundred eggs on these expeditions.

A murre pair whose egg disappears either through predation or accident is likely to re-lay, but not for two to three weeks. If the summer is short that year, the delay may mean the chick will not be big enough to survive autumn storms. Going to sea for murre chicks occurs from mid- to late-August when, still unable to fly, they jump from their ledges to the adults gathered below in the surf. A crying chick swims back and forth until it is adopted and taken out to sea to finish growing accompanied by one of the adults, usually its own male parent.

An unexpected predator of seabirds in the Pribilofs is the Steller sea lion. These tawny marine mammals abandoned their rookery on Saint Paul's Northeast Point and took up residence on Walrus Island, about eight miles east. As recently as 1949 that low, rocky shelf of an island had been recorded as one of the world's largest murre colonies. Now only about 200 murres nest on a sea stack at the island's north end.

The people who make pilgrimages to the Pribilofs for birds come not only for the attraction of masses, but also for the single, wayward bird.

Nick Stepetin, life-long resident of Saint Paul, is their best guide. He glasses the marshes, ponds, and roadsides daily if his schedule permits so he knows just when a new bird arrives and where it was last seen.

What Nick and his cohorts are seeking are birds that pause spring or fall on their way to or from foreign breeding grounds, usually Asia. A sighting of an Oriental cuckoo, Temminck's stint, curlew sandpiper, or eye-browed thrush puts huge smiles on the faces in tour groups that come to the Pribilofs specifically to chase its elusive and unpredictable feathered tourists.

Occasionally the Pribilofs will yield a bird such as the bristle-thighed curlew that tour groups spent time and money looking for, in vain, elsewhere in Alaska.

Craig A. Hansen

Two hundred years of history swirl around the fabulous fur seal herds of the Pribilofs. The islands were discovered during the search for the seals' breeding grounds; Russian and American desire to profit from the great herds led to forced occupation of the islands by Aleuts from the Aleutian Chain.

B.E. Lawhead

A wary fur seal bull does not welcome intruders to his rocky domain at Kitasealogh Beach on Saint George.

The Northern Fur Seal

Seals and Sealing

By Craig A. Hansen

Each spring and summer hundreds of thousands of northern fur seals *(Callorhinus ursinus)*, feeding in Pacific Ocean waters to the south, head north to their breeding grounds on the Pribilof Islands in the Bering Sea. The majority of seals return to the rookery of their birth, thus completing a rigorous seven-month migration in which many have traveled more than 7,000 miles.

There are approximately 1.7 million northern fur seals in the world and the Pribilof Islands are the main breeding grounds for an estimated 1.25 million, 80% of the world population. The remaining 20% breed on Soviet-owned islands in the northwest Pacific Ocean.

The fur seal has physical features remarkably adapted for life in the sea and on land. Its fur is composed of two layers: the inner layer is short, soft, and dense, while the outer layer is made of long, coarse guard hairs. Together these layers comprise a pelt, with more than 300,000 hairs per

Editor's note: Craig Hansen, a National Marine Fisheries Service biologist, was conservation officer at Saint Paul for the 1980 and 1981 fur seal harvest.

Both photos by Craig A. Hansen

Leader of the band, this fur seal bull looks out over an audience of bawling cows and pups on Saint Paul. The bull spends much of his time in the bare area in the foreground.

A harem bull watches over his small harem at Northeast Point Rookery in July.

small, tightly rolled cylinders with a narrow, waxy orifice that keeps water out. Their eyes are large, enabling them to feed in the water at night. Fur seals have 36 sharply pointed teeth, many interlocking, allowing their prey little chance of escape.

The color of a seal's fur varies with age and its activities. Female and young, generally, are gray. However, after a few days on the rookery the fur of breeding females is stained a yellowish-brown by mud and excrement. Pups are shiny black when born but become silvery-gray after their first molt in October. Males more than six years old are predominately brownish-black, but individuals vary and some may be dark gray or reddish-brown. At about six years, males begin to develop a short, bushy mane around the neck and shoulders.

Fur seals vary tremendously in size and weight depending upon age and sex. Newborn pups weigh only 10 to 12 pounds, and males are generally a bit larger than females at birth. Adult seals are among the most sexually dimorphic of mammals. A bull seal may weigh in excess of 600 pounds when he first occupies his territory in late spring, whereas mature females are only one-fifth their size, averaging 95 to 110 pounds. Commercially harvested males, predominately three- and four-year-olds, average 68 and 72 pounds, respectively.

Although fur seals are relatively long-lived animals, their life span probably does not exceed 30 years. A female tagged as a pup in 1956 was sighted on Reef Rookery, Saint Paul Island, nursing her pup in 1981 — evidence that females are still productive at 25 years of age. The oldest male recorded was 17 years old.

Fur seals feed mainly at night because their primary food source — small schooling fish — occupy the upper water layers at this time. Seals will feed on whatever species is available but, in the Bering Sea around the Pribilof Islands, they feed principally on walleye pollock, herring, capelin, and sandlance. When available, squid is also a preferred prey.

The northern fur seal is a wide-ranging mammal

square inch, that is impenetrable by water. Because the fur is so dense, it is also an effective insulator, keeping body heat in and providing protection against frigid ocean waters. When on land, seals would be uncomfortably hot on warm days were it not for their flippers, which are large and free of fur. They act as radiators enabling the seals to keep cool; excess body heat is released by waving a flipper in the air. On days such as these, rookeries are teeming with thousands of seals fanning their flippers.

There are several other features that contribute to the fur seals' survival. The external ears are

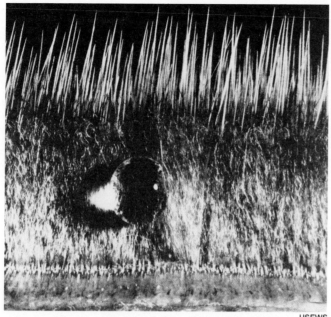

Magnified four times, this cross section of a pelt from a yearling seal shows how the thick underfur repels water and keeps the fur seal dry.

USFWS

with migratory routes extending over vast areas of the North Pacific. In the western Pacific, they migrate from the Soviet-owned Commander Islands in the Bering Sea south to the Okhotsk Sea and the Sea of Japan. In the eastern Pacific, fur seals migrate from the Pribilof Islands to as far south as the Channel Islands off the southern coast of California. International research reveals considerable intermixing between seals from American and Asian islands. Male seals originating from the Pribilofs are harvested each year on the Commander Islands, and a small number of Commander Island seals are taken in the annual commercial harvest on Saint Paul Island. Nevertheless, more than 96% of fur seals found off the west coast of North America originate from the Pribilofs.

The movements of fur seals seldom bring them closer than 10 miles nor farther than 100 miles offshore. They are most abundant between 30 and 70 miles at sea, over the continental shelf. In the open ocean fur seals may occur singly or in small groups,

but an abundant food source tends to concentrate them, and loose groupings of 100 have been observed.

During fall, winter, and spring fur seals are pelagic, remaining at sea to feed and rest. Seals of all ages and both sexes begin leaving the Pribilofs in October with peak departure occurring in early November. Except for adult bulls, who winter in the Bering Sea and Gulf of Alaska, most Pribilof Island fur seals migrate south in the northwest Pacific Ocean. Adult females range as far as southern California by January, but immature animals remain farther north, occupying waters from northern California to British Columbia. The 8- to 10-month-old pups are found in large numbers off California in March through May but are most abundant in waters off the coast of Washington, British Columbia and Southeastern Alaska.

The northward migration back to the Pribilofs begins in February and March. From April through mid-June, large numbers of seals are found in the Gulf of Alaska. Both males and females arrive on the islands in descending order of age; adult males are the first to appear, in late April and early May. Laden with blubber from feeding all winter, the 10- to 15-year-old bulls lumber ashore to occupy a territory, most likely on the rookery of their birth. In years with a late winter, bulls may be seen sitting on ice and snow — undeterred — their primary concern being to establish a territory. Bulls may wait four to five weeks before the cows begin to arrive. During their tenure as a territorial animal, most bulls go without food and water an average of 50 days, but some stay as long as 64 days. By the time they leave in late July, they will have lost as much as 25% of their body weight. Breeding males are subject to high mortality and are able to maintain a territory for three or four seasons at most. It is not unusual to see a dead bull, having succumbed to the physical strain of migration and territorial defense, on the rookery early in June.

Territorial bulls, or beachmasters as some prefer to call them, vigorously defend their territories,

44

which average about 250 square feet, and aggressive displays, roaring, and snorting at neighbors from their boundaries are the rule of the day. Intense fighting occurs, but is infrequent. However, adjacent bulls do manage to inflict wounds on each other, most often around the upper foreflippers and neck. Although these injuries are bloody and appear serious, rarely are they deep enough to penetrate through the blubber layer. The only seals that get into serious trouble are idle bulls or young males that attempt to displace an established bull. At this time the fur seal bull reveals his true ferociousness. All disputes between neighboring bulls appear to dissolve as they focus attention on the intruder. The closest male attacks viciously, slashing or hanging onto the back and neck of the trespasser with his large canines, holding him down. The animal on top often shakes the subordinate vigorously from side to side. If their territory is violated, neighboring bulls will bite at the intruder's flippers and flanks. The challenger may succeed in displacing an established male, but more commonly the animal breaks free only to run a gauntlet of more furious bulls. Once the ruckus ends, the resident bulls promptly return to the business of minding their territories. The trespasser slips into the water to nurse his wounds.

Idle bulls, i.e., adult males, young and old, lacking a territory, are relegated to the hauling grounds or isolated beaches. The hauling grounds are areas near rookeries where non-breeding animals congregate. These animals are joined by the bachelors, sub-adult males ages three to six years, that begin coming ashore in mid-June. The younger males spend a great deal of time sparring and chasing their peers in addition to lounging around. Unlike territorial males, most hauling ground animals make feeding trips to sea at fairly regular intervals.

In August and September those seals coming ashore are mostly two-year-old males and females. They are followed, in October and November, by a few yearlings of both sexes that remain only two or three weeks. Most yearlings and two-year-olds do

Craig A. Hansen

Patrick Kozloff wields a 10-foot bamboo pole while on the bull count, part of an on-going study. The poles are needed to fend off aggressive territorial bulls and to establish the counter's own territory.

not return; they remain scattered across the subarctic waters of the North Pacific for the first year or two of life.

Pregnant females arrive at approximately the same time as sub-adult males. Although the territorial bulls attempt to herd or retain a group of these females, formerly called a harem, the cows actually seek a location rather than a specific bull. Harem bull is a term often used to describe a territorial male because in the past biologists believed that the bull actually acquired the females by herding and keeping them near him, rather than defending a specific area. The term harem, although antiquated, is still commonly used to define a group of females occupying an area defended by a bull. In reality, the most vigorous efforts of a bull are useless if a female is determined to leave his territory. At times, a bull has been observed to lift a cow with his teeth and, with a flip of his head, hurl her backward into his territory after having caught her attempting to leave.

45

The Birth of a Fur Seal

This pup was born at Northeast Point Rookery, July, 1980. The pup's hind flippers appeared first, and about 20 minutes elapsed before the mother completed the birth. The mother seal was very attentive to the pup, vocalizing and sniffing the pup continuously. The final photo shows a second female being curious about the new pup. Some females have been seen trying to steal and defend a pup from its new mother.

1

2

3

Female fur seals are sexually mature at 4 or 5 years, and more than 80% of those 7 to 16 years old become pregnant each year. They return to the rookery of their birth, possibly within a few feet of their own birthsite. Cows tend to occupy areas closest to the water as they come ashore, and due to their natural gregariousness, they are attracted to groups of females. Because of this characteristic behavior, one territory may contain many females whereas another and perhaps adjacent territory has none. Territories with 100 females are not uncommon; however, the average, in 1981, was approximately 35. This uneven distribution may prompt a harem raid or female stealing. A raid may occur when a bull with females in his territory has his attention diverted due to disturbance by an intruder or aggressive display by another bull. A bull without females may use this opportunity to charge into the adjacent territory, snatch a cow in his teeth and carry her to his area setting her down

All photos by Craig A. Hansen

roughly. If he is successful in detaining this female, others may be attracted, and a cohesive group of females may be formed. This stealing behavior is rarely successful, however, because of the difficulty in preventing females from wandering. Additionally, the bull whose area was invaded often grabs the cow being stolen and a tug of war ensues, suspending her in mid-air. The usual result is the initial bull retains the cow, often at the expense of tears in her skin. Cows have reportedly been skinned alive from the brutal tugging of bulls with razor sharp canines.

Within a few hours to several days of their arrival, females give birth to a single black pup; twins are extremely rare. Birth may take place anywhere on a rookery, usually among a multitude of females and pups that seem completely oblivious to what is happening. The pupping season peaks in early July but continues well into August. Four to seven days after giving birth the females come into

Below—Two fur seal pups play at Northeast Point Rookery on Saint Paul. Actually, pups exhibit many of the same behaviors as adults. Here they could be perfecting threat displays similar to adult males' sparring.

Right—A mother seal nurses her newborn pup in July.

Both photos by Craig A. Hansen

48

estrus, which lasts about a day. Mating occurs at this time, usually with the bull in whose territory she gave birth.

After breeding, the female's summer activity alternates between feeding trips at sea and caring for her pup on the rookery. Feeding trips range from 5 to 14 days but average 8, with the female frequently traveling more than 100 miles away. Increased commercial fishing in the vicinity of the Pribilof Islands could very well lengthen the distance females must travel to obtain their food. A pelagic research crew in 1964 found lactating females foraging 250 miles from Saint George Island. If females must travel farther than in the past to obtain adequate nourishment, the chances for survival of the pup may be decreased.

When the fur seal mother does return from the sea, she immediately moves through the rookery seeking her pup. Although females are highly gregarious, most interactions are limited to a few snarls and snaps as they course through the rookery or defend their pups. As the mother wanders about in the area her pup was left, she gives a bleating call and listens for a response. A fur seal mother can distinguish the sound of her pup among a myriad of rookery sounds. Once the responding pup is located, the mother assures herself that it is her own by smell. She nurses only her own pup, roughly rejecting any pup that mistakenly approaches. The female spends approximately a day and one-half to two days on the rookery resting and periodically nursing her pup; nursing continues for three to four months, ending in October.

Fur seal pups must live on their mother's fat-rich milk, and within six to eight weeks of birth they consume a gallon of milk during the two-day feeding. By the time the mother goes off to sea to feed again, her pup is bloated with milk, giving it a pot-bellied appearance. While the mothers are away, the pups sleep much of the time, but also play-fight with peers and scamper among the rocks. Much of their play is similar to adult behavior. This play continues among the subadult males on the hauling ground, possibly as preparation for adult life on the rookery. When pups are not sleeping or playing, they are inevitably scratching. Fur seals, including the pups, have an abundance of mites and lice.

By early August the pups form large aggregations, called pup pods. Pups tend to gather in areas where they are least likely to be trampled by a rampaging bull. In August pups begin to play in and near the water's edge. At first, they are somewhat awkward in their swimming, but they soon gain skill and endurance. They do not have to be taught how to swim as many people believe. They can swim when born but do not voluntarily do so until August. By November, the pups have become proficient swimmers, capable of joining older seals in the migration south.

. . . since 1786

The northern fur seal population has undergone a series of dramatic changes from the time its breeding grounds on the Pribilof Islands were discovered in 1786 to the current period of relative stability. Sealing practices — the taking of fur seals for their thick-furred, luxurious pelts — and changes in herd size and composition have largely reflected management policies and conservation efforts, or the lack of them. Twice the herd was nearly exterminated due to over-exploitation. Management policies ranged from no restrictions to a total ban of the killing of fur seals. The herd went through several rebuilding phases in response to a variety of management schemes. At one point, the population was believed to have reached its peak. To maintain productivity, a deliberate population reduction program was implemented, which necessitated killing females. Ongoing studies of fur seal biology and population dynamics have greatly enhanced the knowledge of wildlife managers. As a result, sealing practices have remained relatively constant the past several decades.

R.H. Day

The breath of these seals vaporizes as the animals are driven to the harvest grounds on Saint George. In earlier times many seals died from overexertion during these drives. Recent practice calls for a short, slow drive which is easier on the seals.

Biologists walk among the fur seals on grassy slopes above Staraya Artil, an unusual rookery on Saint George's north coast. Scientists know of no other fur seal rookery where seals work their way more than 200 feet up a slope away from the safety of the pounding surf.

Douglas W. Veltre

Commercial exploitation of the northern fur seal began with discovery of their breeding grounds. With the major fur resource, sea otters, fast becoming scarce, Russian fur traders immediately turned their pursuits to the fur seal. In the early years of Russian control, fur seals were killed indiscriminately, with no regard for sex, age, or number taken. In the first year, 1786-1787, more than 40,000 fur seal pelts were obtained, while the take of sea otter pelts was only 2,000.

Bishop Veniaminov provided details of the sealing methods used during Russian control. He was stationed in Unalaska during the first half of the 19th century with the Pribilofs in his jurisdiction. According to his account, the soft, fine fur of the silvery-gray pups four or five months of age was the most highly valued, and formed the basis of the industry in early Russian years.

The sealing operation began around the end of September when most pups had molted their black coat. All seals, including females and young, were rounded up and driven to a killing field. During the drive, bulls were separated from the other animals. The young seals and pups were driven as far as seven and one-half miles which required a great deal of time for frequent stops to prevent death by overheating. All the inhabitants (Aleuts), including children, used small clubs to divide the large group of seals into small pods. The seals were then clubbed to death without regard for age or sex. Only one-year-old females were allowed to escape. The men removed and cleaned the pelts with knives. One man could clean the blubber from 50 to 200 pelts per day. Women stretched the pelts over wooden frames and placed them in a drying house to dry over heated stones.

Sealing on both islands was carried on without management because of competition among the many companies to kill as many seals as possible. By 1803, after the slaughter had been conducted for better than 15 years, an accumulation of 800,000 pelts was found in storehouses; 700,000 were proven worthless and discarded at sea.

In 1807, the Russian American Company, a consolidation of Russian fur-gathering companies, finally realized that the continued wholesale slaughter of fur seals would lead to their extermination. To save this valuable resource, they stopped killing seals on the Pribilof Islands. This was the first attempt to conserve and manage the seal herd. But two years later the sealing began anew, and killing was again conducted with extreme negligence. Even bull seals were taken for their pelts, such was the greed of the fur traders. Countless more female seals died on the long drives from rookeries to killing fields.

In the 1820s and 1830s, concern for the seal herd brought about the first real reforms; quotas were established, orders were issued to leave young seals every year for breeding purposes, and neither bulls nor first year pups were to be taken. More care was taken during the drives to ensure that females escaped. But by 1834 the seal population of the Pribilof Islands had reached an all-time low. From 1786 to 1832, more than three million seals were killed on the Pribilofs. Following this crisis, and recognizing a need to maintain the herd, the Russian government prohibited the slaughter of female seals and set quotas for the number of males to be taken. This policy remained law as long as Russia reigned over all the seal islands and, as a result, the herd increased to several million.

With annexation of Alaska in 1867, the United States government took control of all sealing operations on the Pribilof Islands. The United States intended to continue Russia's 35-year policy of sparing females and allowing escapement of some males for breeding. Although the seal herd had grown large enough to sustain annual kills of several thousand males, in the first two years of United States control killing was enormous, nearly 300,000 seals were taken.

In 1869, increased concern resulted in the Pribilof Islands being set aside as a special reservation for the protection of fur seals. The following year, the United States Treasury awarded the

Alaska Commercial Company a 20-year lease to sealing rights. Certain restrictions were imposed that limited sealing to June, July, September, and October and to males older than one year. The annual take was not to exceed 100,000 seals. The company established salt houses for curing pelts at several points on Saint Paul and Saint George, thus eliminating the long drives in practice since the Russian years. During the latter years of the lease, the quota became increasingly harder to obtain because of a marked decrease in the seal herd. Nevertheless, the Alaska Commercial Company succeeded in shipping out nearly two million pelts during their lease. Regardless of the restrictions placed on sealing practices, the herd was still being depleted. This was due largely to the effects of pelagic sealing, the taking of fur seals at sea.

As a commercial enterprise, pelagic sealing began in the late 1860s. Prior to this time, pelagic sealing was limited to Northwest Coast Indians using canoes and spears and, in some cases, gill nets. But this primitive subsistence activity soon turned to a business because of two innovations: the use of mother ships capable of transporting canoes and hunters many miles offshore, and the use of firearms. In the pelagic sealing heyday (1889-1909), more than 600,000 seals were killed, exceeding or nearly exceeding the number harvested on land every year. This depredation was disastrous to the Pribilof herd for three reasons: many seals were lost due to sinking or wounding, most seals taken were breeding or pregnant females feeding at sea, and loss of a female subsequently meant the death of her pup from starvation on the rookery.

In an effort to stop pelagic sealing the United States claimed exclusive control over the eastern Bering Sea, resulting in the seizure of a number of American and Canadian vessels for sealing in these waters. Examination of the pelts revealed as many as three-quarters of the seals killed were females and that many were lactating. The seizures of Canadian vessels sparked a heated controversy

with Great Britain, which was settled by the signing of a treaty in 1893. Thereafter, pelagic sealing within 60 miles of the Pribilof Islands was prohibited; a closed season was established for pelagic sealing from May 1 through July 31; and the use of nets, firearms, and explosives to take seals in the Bering Sea was outlawed. These regulations proved ineffective because females frequently ranged further than 60 miles from the rookeries, and killing was still allowed in August when they were at sea feeding. In addition, skilled Indians using spears and canoes enabled pelagic sealers to circumvent the firearms restriction.

The second 20-year lease was awarded the North American Commercial Company with the same basic features as the previous one. However, its annual quota was reduced to 60,000. Because pelagic sealing was at its peak during this period, the company rarely obtained its quota. During the company's 20-year tenure, it obtained approximately 340,000 pelts while the pelagic take exceeded 650,000.

In the early 1900s, the government's concern for the seal herd prompted initiation of studies to learn more about fur seal biology to improve the effectiveness of seal management. The first real controls stemmed from this research. All four-year-old males were to be spared, a number of two- and three-year-old males were to be marked annually for breeding, and size limits of pelts based on weight were imposed. A move aimed at Japanese pelagic sealers prohibited trespassing on fur seal rookeries. Armed guards were posted at various points around the islands to prevent the sealers from coming ashore.

Further attempts to thwart pelagic sealers led to several desperate proposals, one being to kill as many seals on land as possible, under existing law, to prevent pelagic sealers from getting them. A less radical measure was actually undertaken in which females and pups were hot-iron branded to damage their pelts, in hopes of discouraging pelagic sealers. By 1909, the fur seal population was estimated to

In the early 1900s, foreign poachers sometimes came ashore under cover of fog to get seals. Aleut men organized into watches and patrolled the rookeries to protect the herds. This group was photographed near a watch house on Saint Paul about 1900. The group included (1) Nicolai Kozloff; (2) Mike Kozloff; (3) Innokenty Sedick; (4) Paul Kozevisnikoff; (5) Metrofan Krukoff; (6) Peter Bourdukofsky; (7) George Kochergin; (8) John Krukoff; (9) Zachar Tetoff; (10) Gregory Shaishnikoff; (11) Nicolai Bardanoff; (12) Simeon Melovidov; (13) Stefan Rukovishnikoff; (14) John Merculief; (15) John Fratis; (16) Evanalie Kozeroff; (17) Pireria Pankoff; (18) Jacob Kochutin; (19) Nicolai Krukoff; (20) Nekita Hapoff; (21) Simeon Nozekoff; (22) Peter Oustigoff; (23) Peter Tetoff; (24) John Stepetin; (25) Apalon Bourdukofsky; (26) Nester Kushin; (27) Elary Stepetin; (28) Neon Tetoff; and (29) Karp Buterin.

About 1953 the brine paddle tank replaced the salt curing method on Saint Paul. Placing the pelts in the brine tank required less time and labor.

Reprinted from *Alaska Fishery and Fur-Seal Industries, 1953*, USFWS

Seal skins are hosed down during the 1921 harvest on Saint Paul.

National Marine Fisheries Service

tion, pelagic sealing was prohibited by nationals of the four governments, except by aboriginals using primitive methods. In addition, the convention provided for a sharing of fur seal pelts between participating members: Canada and Japan received 15% of the United States and U.S.S.R. take of land-harvested pelts. Similarly, the United States and U.S.S.R. were to receive 10% of the pelts taken on the Japanese-owned Robben Islands. The convention also declared a commercial sealing moratorium on the Pribilof Islands for five years with the exception of small subsistence harvests by local residents.

Throughout the early years of American ownership of the Pribilofs, sealing managers tried to selectively take certain seals, concentrating on three- and four-year-old males. This was primarily due to the high quality of their fur and to their availability on the hauling grounds in mid-summer. Restrictions regarding age, sex, and quantity taken were imposed to maintain a viable population while allowing a large take of these particular seals. The fur market had developed on the basis of pelts from these animals. In addition, steps were taken to maintain pelt quality after removal from the field. One measure involved curing the blubber-laden pelts in salt (kenching) before sending them to the furrier for blubber removal and further processing. This method prevented the decomposition that inevitably occurred to many pelts prior to their arrival at the fur companies.

The 1920s represented the beginning of a new era in sealing operations; increased studies of fur seal biology and behavior enabled agents to better manage the population as a renewable resource. Changes in harvesting and pelt processing techniques focused on a better quality finished product. Pelts were now washed and cooled in sea water rather than stored dirty in salt. Blubber was removed on the islands rather than at the fur companies. Peeling or stripping the pelt from the seal's body at the time of harvest replaced the slower process of knife skinning.

Fur seal pups are herded together, and each shearer grabs one and clips the fur on top of the head. The pups will later be identified as a percentage of sheared to unsheared to determine the total pup count for the year. Shearers wear leather gloves and sleeves because the pups are very aggressive and bite when picked up.

be just slightly more than 200,000 — the lowest in history. (Recent calculations put that figure at 315,000.) A year later, an Act of Congress outlawed pelagic sealing by United States nationals, prohibited killing females and pups on land, and did away with the leasing system.

In 1911, representatives from the United States, Great Britain (for Canada), Russia, and Japan met to form a treaty which resulted in the North Pacific Fur Seal Convention. Under terms of the conven-

special sealing crew of Aleuts harvested more than 117,000 seals — the largest number killed on the islands in a controlled situation. In 1944 sealing operations resumed as usual and remained unchanged for the next decade.

By 1955, the number of idle bulls equaled the number of territorial bulls. This was due, primarily, to the persistent use of a low limit on maximum body length of harvestable seals. As a result, many young seals escaped the harvest only to become idle bulls later. The herd was not growing, and managers decided to raise the length limit for males and to kill females. The season for females was in August and September when the organized breeding structure was breaking up.

The herd reduction program was expected to improve rearing success of young animals, lower the mortality of pups, and stabilize annual pup production at 400,000. Biologists believed the smaller population would produce a surplus of 60,000 males and 30,000 females, annually. Although females appearing in the drives in 1954 and 1955 were intentionally taken for research purposes, the actual reduction program started in 1956 and continued through 1963. Not since 1847 — the first year females were entirely exempted from the harvest — had females been intentionally killed.

The program was not wholeheartedly embraced. Years of tradition in sparing the females and a lack of knowledge of population dynamics was cause for concern by the local Aleut community and certain federal resource managers. Aleuts and some managers believed that not only was the female and the newly fertilized egg in her body destroyed, but also her newborn pup was left to starve on the rookery. By 1963, the commercial kill of 270,000 females coupled with natural mortality brought the number of females near the desired level of 800,000.

After the reduction program was terminated, females six years old and older having all-white whiskers were allowed to escape the drive. Only females having black whiskers (ages two to four

Except for a few changes, the basic harvesting method has remained constant for more than 50 years. The changes that have been made resulted from concern for the seals. For example, drive lengths were reduced and oversized animals were deliberately allowed to escape to reduce stress and mortality. As a result of these efforts, the seal population grew steadily, reaching a plateau by 1940. In the same year, Japan abrogated the treaty, claiming that an excess of fur seals were damaging their offshore fisheries.

During World War II, the Pribilofs were evacuated and as a result, no harvest was conducted in 1942. However, the following year a years) or a mixture of black and white whiskers (age five years) were taken.

The start of the herd reduction period coincided with the beginning of an unexplained decline in the number of males available for harvest. Scientists speculated that a combination of natural factors in the marine environment, such as predation, disease, and climatic conditions, were responsible. Others pointed to intensive foreign fishing in the seals' feeding grounds; increased presence of contaminants; and discarded netting and debris, in which the seals became entangled and died.

An Interim Convention on Conservation of the North Pacific Fur Seal, ratified October 14, 1957, addressed the problem of the declining number of harvestable males. A four-man Fur Seal Commission was established whose primary objective was to determine the measures necessary to ensure maximum sustainable yield.

The annual harvest fluctuated widely in the 1960s and continued to decline overall. As a result, the North Pacific Fur Seal Commission (NPFSC) recognized the need for further land-pelagic research. In 1973, the NPFSC adopted a proposal that provided new emphasis on fur seal research in the Bering Sea. This research concentrated on collecting seals at sea to compare their feeding habits in the 1970s with those of the 1950s and 1960s. The commission also set aside all of Saint George Island as a research control area with a moratorium on the fur seal harvest for an indefinite period. (Since 1976, a subsistence harvest has been permitted.) The purpose of the moratorium was to compare the growth and behavior of an unharvested population with that of the harvested population on Saint Paul Island.

In the late 1960s and early 1970s animal protectionists were questioning the humaneness of the fur seal harvest. Federal managers responded by contracting with independent groups to study the effectiveness of traditional and alternate methods of stunning and killing fur seals. The Bureau of Commercial Fisheries (currently the National Marine Fisheries Service) initiated investigations of the humaneness of the seal harvest as early as 1968. A five-man team of biologists was organized to experiment with alternate methods of killing fur seals and to review the entire harvesting operation. The team concluded that none of the methods tested were adaptable to harvesting fur seals. The original method of stunning with clubs proved to be the most rapid, efficient, and humane method of harvesting. The independent studies reached the same conclusion.

In almost 200 years of sealing on the Pribilof Islands, the major changes have been of management schemes applied to regulate sealing in response to fluctuations in the number and composition of the fur seal population. Managing a seal herd for harvest while simultaneously attempting to keep the population at an optimum level is difficult and complex. New measures may be required in the near future. During the past decade, the estimated number of pups born each year and the number of males taken in the annual harvest has decreased slightly, indicating that a decline is occurring in the total fur seal population of the Pribilofs.

United States and foreign fisheries have increased tremendously in the Bering Sea, competing with fur seals for food. The decline could, in part, be a response to declining availability of prey. Some people contend that the annual harvest is the cause for the population decline. This is not true because such a small percentage of the total population is taken, and only a small portion of the male population is necessary to fertilize all breeding females. The situation on Saint George Island also refutes the latter notion. Although a commercial harvest is not conducted, the fur seal herd on this island is declining as well. What is more interesting is that, since imposition of the moratorium, behavioral research studies have shown the number of males has steadily increased while the number of females and pups has progressively declined. With fewer females available

In their efforts to better understand the fur seals, government agents came up with a variety of experiments to study the animals. Here (from left) Raul Vaz-Ferreira, an observer from Uruguay; and Karl W. Kenyon, William H. Sholes, Jr., and Robert Zanes Brown, all biologists with U.S. Fish & Wildlife Service, prepare to launch two meteorological balloons from which cameras are suspended to photograph fur seals at Polovina Rookery on Saint Paul Island.

Craig A. Hansen

Left—The observation blind for viewing seals at Little Zapadni Rookery on Saint Paul gives visitors a close look at the famous seals. Zapadni-Tolstoi Rookery is to the right and Otter Island lies on the horizon.

Right—A subadult male fur seal, entangled in a necklace of netting, stands out from the other seals at Zapadni Rookery on Saint George. Sealers usually harvest animals entangled in debris because they think these seals will die painfully from starvation or suffocation.

there will be fewer pups born, and the Saint George seal population may eventually remain consistently smaller than it has been in the recent past. The total population decline could very well be the result of the herd reduction program and the continued policy of killing females considered surplus to the population, as late as 1968. If this is so, then pup births should increase as the herd recovers, in the near future.

In managing the fur seal herd, the federal government has adhered to a policy of harvesting seals considered surplus to breeding requirements. Because fur seals are highly polygamous and the sexes are born in near equal numbers, pelts of young male seals can be harvested for profit without disturbing the rookeries or adversely

affecting herd productivity. The business of harvesting fur seals is likely to continue under federal control at least until 1984, due to international agreement; on October 14, 1980, the United States, Canada, Japan, and U.S.S.R. signed a protocol extending the Interim Convention of North Pacific Fur Seals for four years. However, because of a proposed phase-out of federal involvement in the Pribilof Islands, sealing operations may be taken over by the Tanadgusix Corporation, the Saint Paul village corporation.

The annual harvest can continue as a profit-making business, although with limitations. In fiscal year 1979, the last year when full figures are available, sale of seal skins brought the government a net profit over costs of $500,000. This figure

B.E. Lawhead

represents the total sale of skins obtained in 1979 less all harvesting and processing costs. This margin is lower than previous years because of the depressed market for furs and the increase in processing costs. The seal harvest is more than just a business, however.

Traditionally, during the sealing season, many Aleuts are employed, students have returned from off-island schools, and visits from relatives are frequent. Except for a few biologists and the resource manager from Seattle, sealing is limited to federally employed Aleut men and women. Approximately 45 employees, including 3 women, are involved with the field operations; for the first time in modern history women were hired as part of the seal harvesting crew in 1980. The pelt processing plant provides work for an additional 40 employees, of whom 13 are women. All are paid according to the prevailing federal wage grade in Alaska, but the hourly rate varies according to experience, position, and length of service.

For the past seven years, the commercial harvest on Saint Paul has averaged approximately 25,500 seals. Although there has not been a commercial harvest on Saint George since 1973, a subsistence harvest started in 1976 currently takes an additional 350 seals each year. The methods employed on both islands are the same, although the time frame and number of people involved in each of the harvests varies considerably.

Harvests from the smaller seal population on Saint George have historically produced fewer pelts. In the two years prior to imposition of the moratorium, approximately 9,700 pelts were obtained. In those years, sealers worked three days a week; under the current scheme approximately 13 men harvest 25 seals, twice a week, over a seven-week period. This schedule, beginning in early July and extending well into August, assures a supply of fresh meat through a good portion of the summer, considered important by residents.

The commercial harvest on Saint Paul takes place during five weeks beginning the last week in June and terminating around July 31. The 25-day season consists of five rounds (each week is a round) in which every major haul-out area is harvested once each round. There are several reasons why this mid-summer season has proven to be the most effective. It is biologically sound because, during this time, the hauling grounds are occupied by young males considered surplus to the herd. These males also have the finest coats, free of bites and scars, providing the highest quality pelts. In addition, the harvest terminates prior to the onset of staginess — a condition of the pelt when new guard hairs are coming in and old ones are being shed during molting. Stagey pelts are considered inferior in the fur business.

A typical day of sealing begins at 4:00 A.M. with a sealers-only breakfast at the King Eider Restaurant. As 5:00 A.M. nears, the sealers, in knee-high rubber boots, don their rain gear and climb into pickups or the modified truck known as the sealer bus. Led by the sealer foreman, all vehicles file slowly out of town into the darkness. The train of vehicles travels for 20 to 40 minutes, depending upon which hauling ground is to be harvested.

The procession eases along the road to the hauling grounds, then all lights go out, the truck rolls quietly to a stop and the sealers get out. A small group led by the more experienced sealers moves single file to the beach, through wet, waist-high tundra. Quietly they walk along the sand or among the rocks downwind from the hauling ground. The pace quickens to a trot as they near the main bachelor group. Already, older, solitary, idle bulls have spotted the sealers and charge headlong for the sea. When the sealers are within 50 to 100 yards of the bachelor group, they break into a full run along the water's edge sending the seals inland, preventing their escape to the sea. The seals bunch together as the sealers whoop, whistle, or clap sticks, driving them through the cool, dew-covered vegetation of the subarctic tundra. The distance to the grass-covered killing fields is fairly short, but the seals are given frequent rest periods to reduce stress and avoid heat prostration. Although the seals are herded along much like sheep or cattle, they are not nearly as docile. Sealers are always on the alert for an overly aggressive bachelor that may turn on them or rush for the sea. During the drive, the experienced men use great care in separating out oversized males and bulls, allowing their escape back to the water. This maneuver eliminates unnecessary stress to the seals and possible danger to sealers when it comes time to stun the smaller animals. Once all the seals are herded together on the killing field, the actual harvest begins.

The harvest is the first phase of the two-phase sealing operation. The work is efficiently organized and carefully supervised by the sealer foreman, himself a seasoned sealer, and the resource management specialist. It is conducted one step at a time by rows of men in assembly line fashion. Each group of men, specializing in one procedure, moves to its position only after the previous task has been completed. The organization precludes mixing of steps and the possibility of accidents.

On cue from the sealer foreman, the pod-cutters, young men that must be quick-thinking and fleet-footed, spring into action. Using old stunning clubs placed inside foot-high tin cans, two pod-cutters separate a small group of seals away from the main band. This is done by approaching the seals from opposite sides while rattling the can along the ground with the club. This action divides the seals, leaving a small pod of five to eight animals separated from the larger group. The pod is then *canned* towards the stunners who quickly encircle the animals. Each stunner holds a club in his hands, which is basically a five-foot, elongated bat, traditionally made of hickory. The stunners raise the clubs above their heads and when a seal within the size limit is correctly positioned, it is struck once on the head. The blow is usually enough to crush its thin skull. Occasionally, a second blow is delivered immediately to assure unconsciousness. Oversized males are allowed to escape.

Craig A. Hansen

A typical pod ready to be harvested clusters together on Kitovi killing field. A seal rejected for the harvest sits in the background.

61

A pod-cutter with a can and stunners with clubs raised begin the harvest.

1

The sticker pierces the heart or severs major blood vessels killing the seal instantly.

3

Seals are stunned with a single direct blow to the head which crushes their thin skull.

2

The ripper cuts along the midline of the belly and then around the hind flippers.

4

The ripper makes two quick circular strokes to cut the pelt away from the foreflippers.

5

Members of the skinning crew then move into action. The barman pins the carcass to the ground, while three pullers strip the pelt from the body.

6

Pullers with nippers or clamps strain to remove the pelt.

7

All photos by Craig A. Hansen

8

An overview of the harvest scene shows pelts (foreground), carcasses (mid-ground), stunners, and waiting seals.

An albino fur seal challenges intruders at Tolstoi Rookery. The albino first appeared in July, 1980; it reappeared the next year, again in July. Biologists estimate, based on its size, that the seal was four years old in 1981.

Craig A. Hansen

All males appearing in the drive that are 49 inches or less are harvested. This length has been determined to be the most common for males four years and younger. Prior to the last two seasons, the length was 47 inches, but biologists consider the number of males that have been escaping the harvest more than adequate and as a result managers have raised the upper limit.

Two exceptions to the size restriction are seals that appear in the drive with netting around their neck and seals of biological interest. Each year a few seals appear in the drive entangled in fishing net or other debris such as plastic packaging bands. In the past, only harvestable animals were taken, and all others were either released to the sea or attempts were made to remove the netting material. The latter procedure was dangerous for the men and harmful to the seals. Since biologists think that entangled seals will die painfully by slow strangulation as they grow or by starvation from an inability to swallow food, they are taken regardless of size or sex.

During the harvest of the Tolstoi hauling ground in 1980 and again in 1981, an albino — golden-colored with pink nose, eyes, and flippers — male fur seal appeared in the drive and on the killing field. Biologists estimated its age to be three years old in 1980. Although the albino was well within the size limit, the animal was spared because of its biological interest. Albinos are very rare and for one to obtain the age of three or four is remarkable, since 50% to 70% of all fur seal pups born die in their first year.

After the seals are stunned, they are laid in rows of six to eight. Within seconds a sealer, called a sticker, wielding an extremely sharp knife, pierces the heart or severs the major blood vessels leading to the heart. This procedure, called exsanguination, drops blood pressure to zero, killing the seal instantly. The stunners continue as the skinning process begins behind them. The dead seals are partially skinned by the rippers. These men, using knives honed to a fine edge, make an incision in the belly along the midline to the tail and continue around the hind flippers. The pelt is cut free of each foreflipper with two quick circular strokes. They finish by cutting the pelt away from the head and flipping the seal over on its belly. A four-man team performs the actual skinning procedure. The bar man sets his two-pronged fork into the ground, pinning the neck of the seal carcass down. The other three men, called pullers, grab the pelt at the head with their nippers (clamps attached to ropes), jerk back suddenly, then peel the pelt away from the body.

When the skinning process is completed, a biologist snips the snouts from a representative sample of the carcasses. Early in the 1950s, marine mammal biologist Victor B. Scheffer discovered that the age of subadult seals could be determined by counting the ridges on the upper canine teeth. This procedure was implemented in 1962. Snouts are collected from each day's harvest so that the canines may be extracted and cleaned, and tooth ridges counted to determine age.

The pelts, or skins as they are often called, are laid out to cool fur side down in 10 rows of 5, comprising a block of 50. The entire operation proceeds until all harvestable males are taken. Any system that requires more movement and handling of the seals would cause great stress to the animals and increase the danger to sealers.

Nevertheless, harvesting methods are continually reviewed. Since 1972, the federal government has solicited a veterinarian to act as humane observer each season. The veterinarian observes each day's harvest, and consults with the sealer foreman to ensure that the harvest is conducted humanely and as stress-free to the seals as possible. All travel, food, and lodging expenses are provided by the government. However, the observer volunteers his or her time, thus assuring independence and objectivity in their report, filed at the season's end.

Most sealers take part in throwing the pelts into the skin truck, for transport to the processing plant. Only when the field is cleared of all pelts are the sealers through for the day. Once the pelts have been removed from the seals, the carcasses are used in a variety of ways.

All carcass handling activity takes place a minimum distance of five rows behind the sealing operation, to maintain order and prevent accidents. Resident Aleuts who want seal meat have first rights to take the parts they prefer; livers, hearts, shoulders, ribs, and foreflippers are the most sought after cuts. Almost all residents own freezers, and free seal meat is an excellent way to avoid the cost of high-priced beef shipped in at great expense.

Since there is no commercial harvest on Saint George, the community must rely on a small subsistence harvest. Saint George Aleuts claim a quota of 350 seals provides too little meat. To supplement the subsistence harvest, two Saint George sealers fly to Saint Paul for two weeks to take meat from the commercially harvested seals. They bring with them a list of various cuts of meat requested by each household. For example: in 1980, 2,800 flippers, 340 chests, 400 shoulders, and various other parts were obtained; totaling 8,500 pounds. Hearts and livers were flown fresh the day of the inter-island charter flight, while the remainder of the meat was shipped frozen at a later date.

Tanadgusix Corporation and the National Marine Fisheries Service have agreed to allow the corporation all rights to use the carcasses, so after the meat-pickers have obtained their meat, corporation employees begin their work. Many of the employees are young boys and girls, aged 12 to 17. Former sealers, employed by the corporation, carefully supervise as many as five boys who remove the penis bone *(oosik)* and testes from each carcass. These are sold to an Oriental market, to be processed and resold for medicinal purposes. Other employees move among the carcasses, quickly gutting them with deft strokes of the knife. The entrails are thrown into a trailer and later discarded in an isolated area destined to become fox food. The carcasses are then hauled by truck to the by-products plant, leaving the killing field clean of sealing debris.

The original by-products building, erected in 1918 by the United States government, was located at the site of the present structure on the westernmost edge of town. It was a small reduction plant constructed to render seal carcasses into meal, and into oil from which glycerin — essential material for munitions — could be prepared. The plant was enlarged and modernized several times to achieve the present massive structure, largest on Saint Paul Island. At various times the plant produced meal for fox food (blue fox furs were very valuable at this time and supplemental feeding was an important part of trapping operations), fertilizer, fish food for hatcheries operated by the U.S. Fish & Wildlife Service, and as a protein supplement in the poultry industry. Historically, oil from seal blubber was used by Aleuts as fuel for cooking, lighting, and heating their *barabaras* (sod-covered houses). However, the primary use of seal oil has been for tanning sealskins and other leathers. The by-

John and Margaret Ibbotson

A truckload of minced, frozen seal meat awaits shipment at Saint Paul.

products plant was closed down soon after the 1962 season because of the poor market, rising wage rates, and equipment failure.

In 1964, a five-year contract was awarded to a private firm giving them rights to the fur seal carcasses. The company successfully used most of the carcasses through the entire contract period. In an assembly line manner, the carcasses were hung by hooks on a cooling line, washed, then coarse-ground (bones, flippers, and all), packaged into 50-pound bags, and frozen. An average of 900 tons of ground, frozen meal, labeled sealburger, was produced annually and sold to mink ranchers in Idaho and Oregon to be used as part of a mink food formula. The company renewed the contract and

Workers fill a wagon with salted seal skins at Saint Paul in 1891.

National Archives No. 22-FA-410

continued producing sealburger until 1976. Tanadgusix Corporation leased the company's equipment and produced sealburger in 1977, but it has not been produced since.

In recent years, use of the seal meat has been comparatively low due to equipment failure throughout the plant. Steps have been taken to improve the operation and, in 1980 and 1981, approximately half of the harvested seals were used.

In the present operation, under Tanadgusix Corporation's ownership and control, frozen seal carcasses are cut into chunks, then boxed and shipped frozen. The highest demand is for king crab bait, but hearts, livers, and kidneys are also shipped frozen to be used as sled dog food. Not all carcasses are utilized, however, and some are discarded.

One or two days a week a tour guide, representing Alaska Exploration Holidays and Cruises, escorts a group to the killing field to watch the sealing operation. The trip is strictly voluntary and requires arriving at the harvest scene by 6:00 A.M. All visitors are kept well back from the stunners and must view the operation on the side opposite from where the seals are rejected to prevent disruption of the sealing crew and to protect observers from being harmed by a runaway seal. Some people fail to understand that fur seals allowed to escape do not always move in the direction intended and that errant seals can be very dangerous. Occasionally an animal will scramble past the stunners and charge, bewildered, towards the sealing crew or in the direction of observers. At this point, everyone must stop what they are doing and allow the animal ample space and time to become oriented and move in the direction of the beach.

The last day of sealing is special. In 1980 and 1981, the season ended with the harvest at Reef hauling grounds, closest to the city of Saint Paul. This is, historically, one of the longest harvests and often continues into the afternoon. But after all the pelts are loaded the sealers line up in their trucks behind the sealer foreman. The entire procession, a motley assemblage of 15 to 20 vehicles, parades slowly into town, lights flashing and horns blaring. They roll through town traveling every road as villagers lean out of windows waving white towels. Elderly women stand in doorways and, in the age-old tradition, beat on metal pots with wooden spoons. Others hand out sodas or beer, gratefully accepted, as the trucks slowly pass by. The parade terminates only after cruising past the processing plant, where a couple of men have large hoses ready to douse all vehicles and riders sitting exposed in the truck beds. Many get drenched. But it's all part of the festive mood, and everyone laughs as they head for home to clean up and begin celebrating the end of five, long, strenuous weeks of sealing.

The season, however, is not over for those working the second phase of the sealing operation which takes place at the processing plant. This is strictly a skin-curing operation, where all the necessary steps are taken to preserve the skins, preventing them from decaying until they are processed into quality furs.

The pelts are hauled from the field by truck directly to the wash house, one of four weathered gray buildings that comprise the plant. Two men climb atop the load of pelts and throw them through one of many openings in the side of the building while another employee counts them. The pelts land in a three- or four-thousand-gallon redwood tank of cold water, pumped in from the Bering Sea. Once all the pelts are in tanks — 300 or 400 pelts depending on tank size — they are totally submerged by lowering wooden racks down across the water. The pelts are soaked overnight in the tanks which are drained and refilled periodically. This process cools the pelts down immediately and cleanses them of dirt, blood, and grass.

The following day the pelts are transferred by an overhead steel bucket into the blubbering shed where the blubber is removed. Initially, the pelts are dumped onto a centralized table where

After seal carcasses are brought to the processing plant, they are
cut up, and the meat is stored in bins in a deep freeze.

A worker hooks seal carcasses onto a conveyor at the meat
processing plant at Saint Paul. From 1918 to 1961 most of the
carcasses and blubber were converted to meal and oil at the
by-products plant. About 350 tons of meal and 40,000 gallons of oil
were produced each season and sold to the highest bidder at
Seattle. The meal was used as a protein supplement in animal
feeds, and the oil was used in making soap and in tanning.

Below—Skins that have been washed, cleaned of blubber, cured in saturated salt solution, and drained are rubbed with salt and boric acid powder, rolled, and packed in barrels for shipment.

Right—In back-breaking labor, workers remove all of the blubber and meat from the seal pelts by hand.

Reprinted from *Alaska Fishery and Fur-Seal Industries, 1956,* USFWS

Reprinted from *Alaska Fishery and Fur-Seal Industries, 1953,* USFWS

Workers salt seal skins on Saint Paul in 1953. Prior to the early 1950s, all pelts were cured in this manner.

Reprinted from *Alaska Fishery and Fur-Seal Industries, 1953,* USFWS

A worker washes a fur seal pelt on Saint Paul.

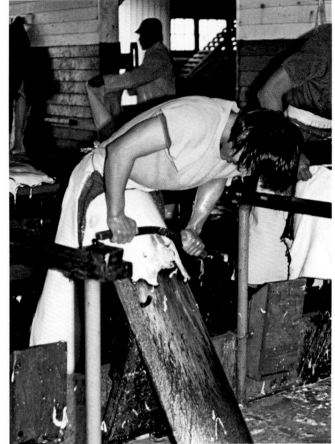

A young Aleut removes bits of blubber and meat from a fur seal pelt during the curing process. After the pelts are washed and soaked in brine, the ears are cut off and the skins scraped clean.

employees using knives cut away the ears. This prevents jamming and inefficient blubber removal when placed into the huge, blue-green blubbering machines. Blubber removal is largely a mechanized process today using two machines, each set for a different thickness for removing blubber from different areas of the pelt. Each machine is equipped with two rollers, one is smooth and the other resembles a push mower blade. The blades of the blubbering machines are dull. The operator grabs a pelt, lays the head end between the rollers, blubber side to the blades, and pushes a pedal that brings the rollers together. With a high-pitched whirr, the blades rub or mulch the blubber from the neck and shoulders of the pelt. A second man repeats the procedure removing the blubber from the lower two-thirds of the pelt. The scrap blubber is pumped into a tank truck and discarded at the blubber dump. The pelts are thrown onto a conveyor that leads to the blubbering men. These men are young and strong; their work is back-breaking. The blubbering knife, a two-handled, curved dull blade approximately 15 inches from end to end, is held as each man grabs a pelt and slings it over a waist-high, convex, metal beam set at a 60° angle. The pelt is smoothed down over the beam, and any

Lael Morgan, Staff

Marsha Melovidov
packs seal skins in
boric acid on
Saint Paul.

Maxim Stepetin
waits amid barrel
after barrel of cured
seal pelts.

blubber remnants left by the machines are removed by rubbing the knife repeatedly across the pelt.

Prior to the first extensive use of the blubbering machines in 1971, all pelts had to be totally hand-blubbered. This required the work of two rows of 15 to 20 young men on the blubbering beams. The present-day process only requires the labor of 10 men, although several thousand skins are still totally hand-worked to remove the blubber in large slabs. These slabs are carted by wheelbarrow to the kenching stalls where they are easily handled when placed into the salt for curing. The cured blubber is eventually shipped to the fur processor, where it is used in the tanning process.

The blubber-free pelts are transported by wheeled table into the brine shed, where the actual curing takes place. The pelts are soaked overnight in three-and-one-half-foot-high, circular, concrete tanks containing a brine solution that is 100% salt saturated. The brine, a mixture of sea water and coarse rock salt, is changed every four to five days to ensure effectiveness in the curing process. The pelts are first placed by hand into a spray-wringer that rinses the fur and wrings the excess water from them. Then, as they are thrown into the tanks, each pelt is submerged by an employee using a bamboo pole, causing the pelt to come into full contact with the brine. Two paddle wheels in each tank periodically churn the brine solution, and wooden racks are lowered over these tanks to keep the pelts totally immersed.

The following morning, two days after the pelts have been harvested, they are removed from the brine tanks and hauled by bucket to the drying shed. Several men and women stack the wet pelts on wooden floor racks, fur side up, in piles of 100 where they are left to drain for five days. Each day a new batch of pelts from another harvest is stacked in this manner. The pelts do not actually dry out; at the end of a week they are still soft, moist, pliable, and ready for boxing, the final process.

Approximately one week from the day they were harvested, the pelts are wheeled from the draining racks and laid out one at a time on the rolling table. An employee grabs a handful of boric acid powder and rubs it over the entire skin side of the pelt. The powder prevents the growth of bacteria, not killed by salt, that would subsequently ruin the pelt. For added insurance a handful of salt is thrown on the pelt before it is folded and rolled into a cylinder approximately a foot in height and eight inches in diameter. The cylindrical pelts are stacked on end into four-foot by four-foot wooden boxes, each holding 250 pelts. All the boxes are stored in a warehouse, for shipment at a later date to Seattle, Washington. From there they are sent by freight train to Greenville, South Carolina, where the final processing of pelts into high quality fur is completed at the Fouke Fur Company. By international agreement, 15% of the pelts, randomly selected, are designated for Canada and Japan. All countries receive their revenue when the finished furs have been sold at the semi-annual fur auctions.

While the plant is in operation, a federally employed conservation officer gives tours three times weekly, an excellent opportunity for visitors to view the entire process firsthand.

Lael Morgan, Staff, reprinted from ALASKA® magazine

The Russian
Orthodox church
dominates this 1891
view of Saint Paul.
Houses for the
sealers form three
neat rows; outsiders
and government
officials conduct
their affairs in
the buildings on
the right.

Under the Double Eagle

Exploration and Development

Vitus Bering's 2nd Kamchatka Expedition in 1741 brought Alaska to the attention of Russia's commercial establishment. When the crew of the wrecked *Saint Peter,* Bering's flagship, finally made it back to Russia after spending a miserable winter in the Commander Islands, the Russian-owned extension of the Aleutians, the furs they brought spurred the first commercial ventures into Alaska. At first the Russians concentrated their hunting on sea otters. Later, however, as otter populations declined, the Russians switched attention to other marine mammals including the northern fur seal.

At the same time, the foreigners set about gaining influence over the Aleuts. Skilled hunters, the Natives were needed by the Russians who sought to enlist the Aleuts' help, first by paying wages and taking advantage of their willing nature, and second by outright conscription when conflict broke out. The invaders soon established hegemony over the Aleuts, who were treated much like the serfs in Russia.

The Russians and their Aleut hunters paid increasing attention to the fur seals as they passed through breaks in the Aleutian archipelago on their spring and fall migrations. If they could discover where the mammals came ashore, hunting would be greatly simplified and fur harvests would skyrocket. Nearly two decades after the Russians extended their explorations throughout the Aleutians and onto the Alaska Peninsula, Gerassim Pribilov, navigating the *Saint George* through

Bering Sea fog to the sound of bawling fur seals, came upon the long-sought breeding grounds in 1786. He named the island Saint George after his ship.

Pribilov himself returned to the Aleutians, but he left a few crew members behind on Saint George to spend the winter. The following spring, in 1787, while exploring the high bluffs on the north side of Saint George, the sailors spotted another island about 40 miles to the northwest. The crew set out by boat to explore this new island, named Saint Peter and Saint Paul in honor of favored saints, but now known simply as Saint Paul. Although Pribilov found no sign of human activity on Saint George, when his crew came ashore on Saint Paul, they found ashes and parts of a pipe and knife. No other record has been found to identify these unknown visitors.

Pribilov was employed by the Lebedev-Lastochkin Company, one of many trading companies competing for a fortune in furs. As competition intensified, the Russians pushed the Aleut hunters to kill more and more seals until populations of these mammals also started to decrease. To bring order out of the chaos created by unbridled competition, Czar Paul in 1799 granted the Russian American Company exclusive jurisdiction over Russian interests in the new world, including the Pribilofs.

Like Pribilov before them, officials of the Russian American Company imported Aleuts from Unalaska and Atka in the Aleutians to harvest the Pribilof fur seals and process their pelts. At first these workers returned to the Aleutians at the end of each harvest. Gradually, however, the Aleuts remained on the islands year-round, establishing villages on Saint George just east of Staraya Artil rookery on the north coast, and at Zapadni on the south coast. The hunters also built a few sod houses at Garden Cove on the southeast shore.

Over on Saint Paul, settlements began at Big Lake and other locations along the north shore. When the Russian American Company took control of the islands, they consolidated all the settlements on Saint Paul at Polovina. To make it easier to ship the furs, these Aleuts were moved, in 1825, to the present site of the city of Saint Paul near Village Cove on a small peninsula jutting from the island's south shore.

Difficulty in hauling seal pelts from the harvesting area to Garden Cove, Saint George's best anchorage, brought about consolidation of the island's villages about midway on the north shore. This location, while convenient to seal rookeries, meant a hazardous journey between ship and shore when arriving and leaving the island.

As competition among the trading companies ended and the routine of harvesting the seals became better established, the Aleuts and Russians worked out living arrangements in the Pribilofs. The latter acknowledged their dependence on the Aleuts' labor: official company policy required half of all Aleut males between 18 and 50 to work for the Russians for a wage one-fifth of what the average Russian worker earned. In reality, the Russians forced nearly four-fifths of the men to work. And while the Czar placed a three-year limit on the time Aleuts had to work for the sovereign, commanders in the field generally ignored the time limit. For their part, Aleuts came to depend on the Russians for certain food items such as sugar and tea, they learned the Russian language, adopted Russian names, and embraced the Russian religion.

In 1824 Siberian-born Ioann Veniaminov arrived in Unalaska as the Russian Orthodox priest for the Aleutians and Pribilofs. A man of remarkable talent who became Bishop of Alaska and later Metropolitan of Moscow, Father Veniaminov inspired hope and new faith among the Aleuts, encouraged their education, and worked out an alphabet and grammar for the Aleut language using the slavonic characters of Russian Orthodoxy. Once they had an alphabet, the Aleuts could learn to read and follow the mass. And by joining the church, they were freed from paying taxes to the Russian government for three years.

Far left—Houseposts indicate that a *barabara* once stood on this site at Northeast Point on Saint Paul.

Left—Traditional hunting implements, such as this bone spear point, have been found on both islands.

Both photos by Douglas W. Veltre

Russian overlords never had lived in the Pribilofs in great numbers. According to Dorothy Jones in *A Century of Servitude: Pribilof Aleuts Under U.S. Rule* (1980), by 1818 only 400 Russians were in the entire Aleutian district which included the Pribilofs; at the time of United States purchase in 1867 the Russians numbered only 812.

From time to time Russians sent Aleuts or Creoles of mixed Aleut-Russian heritage back to the homeland to be educated, then to work as interpreters for the early explorers. Later these Creoles became storekeepers, navigators, priests, and teachers, and assisted in the administration of the islands.

Along the Aleutian Chain the Aleuts continued primarily as pelagic hunters of marine mammals and were able to hone traditional subsistence skills when they were not hunting for the Czar. But in the Pribilofs they were confined to working at some aspect of the land-based fur seal harvest. The Pribilof people no longer had an opportunity to practice talents which had ensured their survival in the Aleutians.

77

Even though the Russian government, through its charter to the Russian American Company, had mandated humane treatment for the Aleuts and granted the Natives Russian citizenship, Aleut populations declined inexorably under Russian control. As Dorothy Jones notes, famed anthropologist Aleš Hrdlička estimated that fewer than 1,900 Aleuts of a population of 12,000 survived Russian occupation in the Aleutians. And the enforced resettlement to the Pribilofs contributed to the decrease. Many Pribilovians, brought from Unalaska or Atka, left a gap in the food-gathering abilities of their former villages and then could not survive the rigors of their new life on Saint Paul or Saint George.

If the population of indigenous hunters was declining, so too was their prey. Sea otters were nearly gone; fur seals and sea lion populations showed diminished vitality. To stem this alarming trend, the Russians instituted conservation measures. However, these efforts could not restore the Russian American Company's earlier profitability.

The less profitable future of the Russian American Company certainly was among reasons which prompted the Czar to look around for a buyer for his new world colony. Supporters of a United States purchase pointed to the riches, including fur seals, to be acquired with the territory. After much debate, the United States bought Alaska for $7.2 million, and from 1867 America claimed jurisdiction of the Pribilofs.

Under a New Flag

The first two years of American control over the islands saw uncontrolled fur seal hunting.

By 1869 government concern for the seals prompted Congress to pass the 1870 Act to Prevent the Extermination of Fur Seals. Provisions of this legislation made the federal government responsible for maintaining, educating, and protecting the Pribilof people. Alaska Commercial Company had control of the seal fishery for 20 years. In return, it had to pay the federal government $55,000 a year in rent plus $2.625 for every seal harvested.

Alaska Commercial Company fell into disfavor toward the end of its 20-year stint, and the second lease was awarded to North American Commercial Company. But once again the seal populations were declining, and the new company did not earn the great profits garnered by its predecessor. At the end of the second lease, in 1910, the federal government decided to take direct control of the fishery.

Editor's note: Not "all" managers or "all" teachers were either brutal or inconsiderate of Aleut feelings. That there was much arrogance in much administration . . . as there might well be in most "far from the bosses" bureaucracies is likely true, but our research and personal acquaintance with a number of early administrators and teachers leads us to believe the following alleged facts are at least to some degree overstated and the reader should take this into consideration. (See Introduction.)

Robert G. Henning

From 1910 to the 1940s government agents, by manipulating seal harvest jobs, dictated many aspects of the Aleuts' lives: agents restricted access to the islands and threatened deportation of Aleuts who dissented; agents destroyed the remaining elements of Aleut culture and prohibited those aspects of Russian culture which the Aleuts had adopted such as language; agents interfered in Aleut marriages and in the traditional custom of adopting relatives.

Official policy discouraged use of the Aleut language. For example, teachers put offensive medicine in the mouth of students caught speaking Aleut. The parents of truant children were punished by locking the father in a basement with only bread and water to eat; the students them-

Above—When the government took over complete control of the Pribilofs in 1910, federal agents set about organizing medical facilities on the islands. Agents decided to convert a small building used for storing salt into a hospital. In August, 1914, these men were recruited to move the building 200 yards to a new location on the main north and south street of Saint Paul.

Left—Resembling a smaller version of Saint Paul, Saint George too has its neat rows of workers' houses and a Russian Orthodox church towering on the skyline in this 1891 photo.

In 1914 Auxenia Stepetin, age about 75, was the oldest Aleut in the Pribilofs.
The Aleut population of the Pribilofs and Aleutians declined drastically under Russian
sovereignty, and the drafty houses constructed for them on the Pribilofs did little to
improve their health.

selves were locked in a closet upstairs with bread and water. Managers hoped to assimilate Aleuts into the American school, but education was limited to six grades on Saint Paul, five on Saint George.

Under Russian control and in the first years of American jurisdiction, Pribilof people received a wage comparable to other workers of a similar classification. But as the American administration tightened its hold on the islands, wages did not keep up with raises earned by other American workers. The Aleuts were usually paid in goods and supplies rather than in cash. They earned cash through sealing and foxing bonuses. In some years the government canceled these bonuses.

Even though they were paid in goods, in the early days Aleuts could choose from supplies on hand at the village store. Later, officials specified how the storekeeper was to fill the grocery bags collected by the head of each household every Saturday morning. Dorothy Jones records the experience of one elderly Aleut:

One day I picked up my bag of groceries. We got only two cans of tuna fish, number 2 size, that was our whole supply of meat for a week. It was my wife's birthday. So I thought, what the heck, we'll have a party and use both cans. We ate potatoes and rice for the rest of the week.

Meat from the cattle and sheep kept on the islands went mostly to the white inhabitants. Only on Christmas and Easter did the Pribilovians sometimes get beef.

Although they worked for the federal government, the Pribilof people did not receive the benefits accorded other federal workers. Social security did not reach the islands until the 1960s.

For Aleut women who had to work, the situation was no better. Only men participated in the sealing and foxing. According to Dorothy Jones, working women were restricted to "midwifery at $5 per delivery, nurse's assistant at the hospital for . . .

In 1920 workers fought their way through tundra and bog to cut a road from Saint Paul to Northeast Point. This convoy of two tractors and a road grader (behind tractor at far left) was working near Polovina when the tractor on the left became stuck. One worker is shoveling away dirt to help free the wheel.

Decked out in their Sunday best, these Aleuts line up for a portrait in front of Old Glory on Saint Paul in 1914.

35 cents for a twelve-hour day (in 1937) and . . . housework in the homes of whites.''

On the islands social contact between Aleuts and whites was discouraged. Teachers were threatened with dismissal for visiting with Natives. Downstairs at the theater was reserved for whites; Aleuts had to sit upstairs. In 1938 the Recreation Hall was put off limits to Aleuts.

Marriage, family adoptions, family quarrels, every aspect of Aleut life came under the regulating arm of the Bureau of Fisheries. Even card playing did not escape, for in 1938 Agent John Lipke posted the following notice in Saint Paul:

ALL NATIVES TAKE NOTICE

Beginning today all card playing will terminate promptly at 10:45 P.M. There will be no card playing, or the playing of other games, in native houses or in any other place after that hour. The recent epidemic of sickness has been attributed directly to loss of rest resulting from late card games. In the event the above orders are disregarded, card playing at night will be prohibited entirely.

World War II interrupted the quiet existence of the Pribilof people with a calamity of major proportions: enforced resettlement by American protectors. Once again the Aleuts were removed from their homes.

Following Japanese invasion of Kiska and Attu in the western Aleutians, the U.S. Navy landed at Saint Paul June 14, 1942, to remove the islanders to Southeastern Alaska. The next day Navy personnel picked up the Saint George Aleuts. The Pribilof people had no warning of the evacuation and were allowed to take with them only what they could carry in their arms. The Pribilof people were interned at Funter Bay on Admiralty Island in Southeastern Alaska: Saint Paul residents were housed at an abandoned cannery, Saint George Aleuts across the bay at an old mine. Conditions were crowded, blankets hung from the ceiling provided the only family privacy, food was scarce, the

Courtesy of Michael Lekanof

Victor Misikin, Father Theodosius, and Nick Mandregan stand in front of a *bidarka* frame from which the skin has been removed for repairs at the Saint Paul encampment at Funter Bay.

fuel supply inadequate, medical personnel overworked and seldom available. For the first year of internment, officials refused to acknowledge the plight of the Pribilovians, and many Aleuts died from these harsh conditions.

In 1940 the U.S. Fish & Wildlife Service had been assigned responsibility for the Pribilof program. These officials sought to control the Pribilovians at Funter Bay, but events in the world beyond their remote home could no longer be kept from them. Even though threatened with banishment, some islanders made their way to Juneau to work for the war effort. The United States Employment Service welcomed these new recruits and opposed Fish & Wildlife's efforts to restrict the islanders.

The price of fur skins increased during the war, and officials did not want to miss the 1943 harvest even though their laborers were interned more than a thousand miles from the harvest grounds. Agents coerced — by threatening that they would never see their home islands again — some of the Pribilovians

The entire Aleut population of the Pribilofs was evacuated from the islands in 1942 after Japanese invasion of the western Aleutians. The islanders were taken to Funter Bay on Admiralty Island in Southeastern Alaska. Saint Paul residents were detained at an old cannery; Saint George residents at an abandoned mine. This photo shows the Saint George encampment; buildings labeled three and five were bunkhouses, building four was the mess hall.

This aerial view shows Saint George before the disastrous fire of June 8, 1950, which destroyed most of the buildings in the foreground including the machine shop, garage, and all of the building and most of the equipment and supplies used for curing and barreling seal skins.

The Pribilofs have been the subject of several films and a few full-length movies. With the movie, *The Seal Islands,* Walt Disney began his famous True-Life Adventure series. Here actors and crew await their cue during filming of *The World In His Arms* in 1952, starring Gregory Peck, Ann Blyth, and Anthony Quinn. Many islanders had parts in the movie including (from left) Eddie Merculief, Alexander Melovidov, Tracy Mandregan, Afrikan Krukoff, Harry May, Matfey Fratis, Terenty Philemonoff, Alexay Stepetin, Dave Fratis, John Kushin, and Stefan Lekanof. An unidentified man leaning against the far boat was the stand-in for Gregory Peck.

into joining sealing crews and transported them back to the islands for the 1943 harvest. In May, 1944, when the Japanese retreated from the western Aleutians, the Pribilof people returned to their fur seal islands.

Back home, they found their houses in shambles, their belongings gone or vandalized. One elderly Aleut recalls sitting in his house under the light of one bare electric bulb when an official came by to chide him for not observing the blackout. When told to put blankets over his windows, the Aleut could only respond that he had no blankets. They had all been taken from the house.

After the war, government officials tried to restore the colonialism which had been the cornerstone of their pre-1945 policy. But internment and contact with outsiders had permanently altered the Pribilovian's attitudes and willingness to tolerate such treatment. The two years spent at Funter Bay also brought their plight to the attention of high government officials above the Fish & Wildlife Service.

Gabriel and Elary Stepetin, brothers, spearheaded efforts to bring reform to the Pribilofs. They urged Saint Paul Aleuts to form a tribal council under the Indian Reorganization Act of 1934. The council hired attorneys and filed a land claims suit in 1951. Not until 1978 was the suit settled, when the Indian Claims Commission awarded $11 million to the islanders. When the Department of Justice contested this figure, the Pribilof people and government representatives compromised with an award of $8.5 million. But by early 1982 the government still had not paid with the money.

Self-government was not the only change slowly working its way into the Pribilofs. In 1950 the government instituted a new wage plan in response to pressure from the islanders. The workers were given Civil Service status with a commensurate annual wage, plus the sealing bonus. Sale of seal pelts still provided the funds for these payments. As always, non-workers were issued supplies.

The 1960s saw a major switch in management policy from control of even the smallest details of Pribilof life to encouragement of self-sufficiency among the Pribilovians and gradual government withdrawal from island life. The fur seal harvest had become unprofitable and maintaining the Pribilovians uneconomical, so managers wanted to limit their operations to the sealing.

Administrators did what they could to aid the Pribilovians in developing new skills. They hoped to integrate the Natives into management of the islands and at the same time prepare them for life on the mainland. The government wanted to move the Saint George people to Saint Paul, and eventually to move the entire Pribilof population to the mainland. Agents burned the houses on Saint George of those families that did decide to move to Saint Paul so that the families could not return. Wages were raised, but the number of work hours and number of jobs decreased.

C. Howard Baltzo, agent in charge during the 1960s, encouraged social interaction between the Pribilof Aleuts and whites. Restrictions on travel to and from the islands were lifted. Management did not prevent the Assembly of God church from establishing a mission at Saint Paul to promote religious diversification.

Alaska Senator Bob Bartlett came to the Pribilofs in 1965 for a firsthand look at the islanders' situation. As a result of his visit, of editorials in the *Tundra Times,* and of pressure from within and outside the Aleut community, the Fur Seal Act of 1966, also known as the Bartlett Act, transferred the houses and much government land to Pribilovian ownership; provided the means for Saint Paul

In the 1960s, conditions improved for the Aleuts of the Pribilofs. Senator Bob Bartlett visited the islands in the mid-1960s. As a result, Congress enacted legislation which finally gave the Pribilof people equal status with other Americans. In 1971 Senator Ted Stevens (right) met with Pribilof leaders. Sitting on the Senator's right is Gabriel Stepetin, long-time Aleut leader who was instrumental in bringing about reforms on the islands in the 1950s and 1960s. Sitting across from the Senator are (from left) Ignaty Hapoff, Terenty Philemonoff, Jr., and Audrey Mandregan, Sr. The two men sitting with Gabriel Stepetin are not identified.

Steve McCutcheon

and Saint George to incorporate as towns under Alaska law; and recognized retirement benefits for those Aleuts who had worked for the government prior to 1950. In line with the Bureau of Commercial Fisheries' plan to disengage itself from the islands, the Public Health Service took charge of health care on the islands, and the State of Alaska took control of education. In short, the Pribilof people became, and were treated as, full citizens of both the United States and Alaska.

By the end of the 1960s, colonialist policies which dominated the Pribilof Island Program the preceding century had given way to progressive withdrawal and consolidation on the part of the federal government, thus increasing independence and responsibility for the Pribilof people.

85

Mother Nature's Christmas Present

By C. Howard Baltzo

This 1966 view of Saint Paul shows the addition of Lake Saint Paul, when the forces of nature momentarily joined together to reshape Saint Paul Island's topography. Village Cove is beyond the buildings on the right.

After spending the summer as usual overseeing the hurly-burly of sealskin harvests on Saint Paul and Saint George islands, I and my wife, Ann, returned in mid-October to devote a year to matters other than fur seals. We were pleased with the arrangement. Not only was the official assignment a stimulating challenge, but previous summers had shown us a wide variety of fun things to do on our personal time. Instead of the forbidding sea-girt rocks the Pribilofs appear on first sight, they encompass sights and satisfactions enough to fill a lifetime for a person in tune with both nature and people. Thrills of discovery, adventure, and achievement never seemed to end. As a good example, let me tell you about our Christmas!

To begin with, the yuletide was plenty long. While still devoutly loyal to their Russian Orthodox holy week beginning January 10, the Aleuts enthusiastically observe the Christian version as well. As throughout bush Alaska, Christmas preparations started in October with sending away for gifts from mail order catalogs. Packages trickled in to Saint

Editor's note: The 1960s were a watershed for the Pribilof Islands. C. Howard Baltzo, director of the Pribilof Island Program from 1960 through 1968 was the first program manager to live year-round in the islands, and instituted many changes in island administration. Here Howard recalls the Christmas season on Saint Paul in 1966 when nature added a memorable touch to the holiday festivities.

Paul on the weekly flights, but delivery to Saint George, 40 miles away, was much more complicated, particularly in the case of radios, clocks, and other breakables. Saint George as yet had no airstrip, so mail drops were made on the infrequent occasions when favorable weather and a willing Reeve or Coast Guard pilot were available at the same time. Everyone made a game of it as the villagers spread out a tarpaulin marked as a target. Bull's-eyes were not uncommon, but at least one full mail bag drifted away to sea.

Cards to friends on the mainland had to be mailed before December if you wanted the recipients to know which year they were intended for. Preparations simply had to be made well ahead of time. As a result, the three normally hectic weeks before Christmas itself were for us a comparatively dull exercise in waiting.

We introduced three novelties of our own to the customary festivities. Anticipating the problem of having a Christmas tree on Saint Paul Island where the only trees were prostrate willows, we shipped a tubbed spruce which had decorated our Seattle sundeck for years. It was soon dubbed the Pribilof National Forest. Secondly, the last plane before the main event brought a large box of tropical blossoms from a friend in Hawaii. He enclosed a card, "Hope this makes it." They did — unmarred through frost, freeze and blizzard. Anthuriums, birds of paradise, and ti graced the office reception desk for weeks, tantalizing everyone. Thirdly, by planning long ahead, we had a fireworks display to usher in the New Year. I had been on the Fourth of July Committee at Wrangell in Southeastern Alaska in the mid-1940s and passed on my expertise to local apprentices.

Our daughter, Dorothy, wrote that she would take advantage of the holiday recess at the University of Alaska at Fairbanks to join us. She had spent the summers of 1960, 1961, and 1963 on the islands with us and especially looked forward to renewing her friendships with the Aleut younger set.

It was Mother Nature, however, who highlighted the program of special events. The Pribilofs are no stranger to storm, and we inhabitants usually took it in stride. But this Christmas Eve a gale made houses not only screech but shiver. Pieces of eaves trough and roofing blew away; clamor rose and fell but never ceased. Glancing over the village on Christmas morn from our house on the hill, Ann startled me into wakefulness by gasping, "Good Lord, what's happened?" An entirely new vista lay before us; the 50-acre expanse of flat grassland reaching from lagoon to ocean was now a lake. Road and ball field were submerged, the lowest row of houses had become a necklace of islands, and a spectacular surf was adding more substance to the flood.

Closer inspection in hip boots revealed a small canyon being cut through the sand dunes into Salt Lagoon on the lee side. The severe storm had coincided with an exceptionally high tide during the wee morning hours to push the Bering Sea above beach line so violently that huge drift logs and barrel-sized boulders were washed inland for considerable distances. Fortunately, the newly forming drain on the other side of Lake Saint Paul gradually lowered the water level and reduced what seemed at first a major calamity to merely an assortment of inconveniences. Not all grim, either. Witness this example.

A leading villager who lived in one of the partly submerged houses had celebrated Christmas Eve per widespread custom and had prudently decided to spend the night with relatives on the hill. Along about noon he drove up in front of the store and joined a group of us still trying to assess the magnitude of our problem. At a logical pause in the deliberations he remarked, "I better be getting home," jumped in his car, drove down the road, and to our utter amazement drove out into the lake until window-deep water stalled his engine. So great is the force of habit.

In the brief but sunlit afternoon Dorothy and I walked the shoreline of our newly acquired curiosity. Couldn't stroll along the road — had to use a hillside. Approach to the East Landing for boats was blocked with a mess of driftwood, kelp, debris, and basalt rock. The scoria-topped driveway to Reef sealing grounds had been scoured by cresting and draining surf. Even a few glass balls were floating in stands of tall beach grass. The new missionary's flooded church earned the sobriquet Chapel-in-the-Sea. We just didn't seem able to get over the surprising change in the overall appearance of the village. "You know," Dotty remarked, "I sort of like the lake there. I think you should keep it."

Instead of joining our walking tour, Ann had returned home to prepare a holiday dinner of baked salmon. For dessert and coffee, we decided to go into the living room. There, overlooked all day, the resplendent Christmas tree surprised us in its colorful ring of yet unopened packages. Despite distractions of the day, we could end it in the traditional serenity of a family gift exchange.

As for Lake Saint Paul, drainage into Salt Lagoon lowered it sufficiently within a few days so that the roadway became exposed, and village life returned pretty much to normal. Then over a course of several weeks the remaining water seeped through the bottom, thereby scuttling comic plans for trout stocking and enabling resumption of baseball in favorable weather. There were periods, however, when the pond served as a usable ice rink.

Not Exactly Main Street

By Regina and Bill Browne

. . . in 1964

Little Saint George is truly the place for anyone who doesn't like to write letters and would like to get away from it all. We certainly cannot say it is primitive living, but it is isolated. We don't have to haul water, or crank up a light plant, or run outdoors in the wind to the little house, but believe us Saint George is far removed from the outside world of Alaska.

Start by looking at a map of the world and locating the Pribilof Islands. Now, imagine a boat arriving just five times a year. Average this out and it really doesn't seem so bad — after all that's a boat every 10 weeks. But it does not average out that way because three of those boats come between May and September. Now, average out the rest of the year with the other two boats.

Yes, you say, but I know for a fact that Reeve Aleutian Airways flies in once a week to the Pribilofs, and there is a Coast Guard LORAN Station, and a weather station out there, so you can't be as isolated as all that. True. There are all these

Editor's note: The Brownes first went to the Pribilofs as teachers on Saint George in 1964. They moved back to the mainland in 1966 and returned to the islands, this time to Saint Paul, in 1968. They left again in 1971 only to return a third time in 1974 for their final four-year stint. This material which describes the Brownes' stay on Saint George originally appeared in a slightly different form in the March, 1967, issue of ALASKA SPORTSMAN®, now ALASKA® magazine. The Brownes now live in Palmer, Alaska, where Bill teaches elementary classes and Regina is a school administrator.

things — at Saint Paul Island, the larger and more northerly of the two inhabited islands in the Pribilof group, but not on Saint George.

The summer is beautiful on Saint George with its myriad of flowers, birds, and seals. Flowers appear in the rolling landscape everywhere. They seem to have little or no smell and are precious miniatures.

The island bustles with activity from May until September. The teenagers are home from Edgecumbe, Wrangell, or Chemawa high schools, and college students are home from everywhere. The sealing crews are at work with the clubbing, blubbering, brining, and packing of the skins. There are tourists, visitors, dignitaries, Bureau of Commercial Fisheries people, biologists, and geologists popping on and off the island. [When the Brownes wrote this article, the Bureau of Commercial Fisheries was part of the U.S. Fish & Wildlife Service; several years ago the bureau was reorganized as the National Marine Fisheries Service.] The M.V. *Pribilof* arrives in May and stays until late June. It returns to Seattle for a few weeks and arrives back in the Bering Sea area for all of August and part of September.

There are dances, hikes, picnics, beach parties, and movies to be enjoyed by the Aleut residents, young people and visitors on the island. With the *Pribilof* running back and forth between Saint Paul, Saint George, and the Aleutian Chain, mail is received and sent out weekly on Saint George. There are also other vessels in the area — supply ships, research vessels, etc.

September comes and the students leave; new

From the bluff, the Brownes had this view of the Russian Orthodox church on Saint Paul and East Landing in the distance in the late 1960s.

teachers arrive and the first to eighth graders start school on Saint George again. The temporary sealers from other parts of Alaska return to their homes. The ever-constant summer sounds of rock 'n' roll from pocket transistors and phonographs through open doors, mopeds and scooters buzzing around, young people shouting, baseball bats cracking, and the *maa-maa-maa* background of the seals diminishes, and once again Saint George is aware of the sounds of the incessant surf from this cold, cold Bering Sea and the mewing of the gulls.

It is October and the boat has gone until late November. Two months. Not too long. We have frantically sent out a Christmas order on the September boat and are wildly hoping we haven't forgotten anything. No more outgoing mail except by wire. Friends and business contacts have been apprised of the mail situation, and you recklessly assume you will not get any bills that will be boldly marked PAST DUE before the November boat.

The days get colder and shorter fast. The temperature becomes 35° to 45°. Later in the winter it will get colder, but not usually any lower than 15° or 20°. It's that wind!

School gets going well. The ground is brown and yellow. The wild celery become brown and brittle, and the children use them for swords or blowing through like giant straw. The mossberries are ripe and make good pies, or just good eating when you are out walking. The killing grounds from summer sealing still smell strangely, and we try to avoid them.

We hope for nice weekends and often get them. The summer mists are blown away, and there are lots of crisp, blowy days. Beachcombing is good — there's a potpourri of Russian and Japanese glass sea balls, or floats, bottles with Japanese and Russian writing, sponges, nets, shells, small Japanese barrels, and if we're lucky, a large sea ball or piece of ivory tusk.

There are shows twice weekly in the evening, and a dance about once a month. We begin to wish

Bill Browne

Passengers load and offload into *baidars* at Saint George after a four-hour trip from Saint Paul aboard the M.V. *Pribilof* in 1965. Today Pribilovians most frequently travel between islands by plane.

we had brought more books and reading material and get anxious for an air drop. If weather is good and luck with us, there will be an air drop about every three weeks. If things don't go right, and the weather is foul, we might go for five or more weeks with no mail.

It seems like it's always a beautiful day when there is a mail drop. Everyone had been buzzing about a drop all morning and now . . . r-r-r-ommm. Stop and listen. A truck going by? The waves? Nope, the Coast Guard. Great Day. Run to the windows, run outside, run up the hill. Look how close the first bag is to the target. Ah, sweet mail. You just can't imagine how wonderful and beautiful U.S. Postal Department green and tan and orange bags can be. Lots and lots of bags.

The day is infinitely brighter. Letters . . . magazines. When we get tired of our magazines, we can exchange with someone else. Naturally, there is the bill marked OVERDUE. I told them and told them. . . .

Halloween. The seals are almost all gone now. We begin to talk of the boat and Thanksgiving and hope that the *Pribilof* will get here with fresh produce for Thanksgiving dinner.

The *Pribilof* is on her way. Five days . . . four . . .

91

Bill Browne

Bill Browne

For many years the M.V. *Pribilof* served as the main supply ship for the islands. When the ship anchored off East Landing at Saint Paul, the community's small motorboat towed a *baidar* out to help ferry supplies back to shore.

Christmas and New Year's on January 7 and 14. We get to celebrate for four weeks. The people out here are good cooks, and we gorge ourselves on the most wonderful holiday pastries and foods. Just think back to when you were a child and imagine the pure ecstasy of two Christmases. And presents at both.

After Christmas and New Year's the months seem to get a little longer. The days are still short and dark and often too windy to venture far. If it does let up a little, we get out hunting and beach-combing. Sea lions and hair seals are abundant. It's easy enough to shoot them, but getting them in from the water after you have killed them seems to be a problem. People have told us that hair seals don't sink when they are shot, but we surely don't know where they go because they aren't there. We do make a *dog* (sea-dog) to use to bring in the seals. The *dog* is a piece of wood with large hooks embedded in it. Attached to a long rope, the *dog* can be thrown out to hook the seal or sea lion and drag it in.

Seal liver is excellent. Sea lion meat is very good, and we have found the skins — if not too scarred — to be quite attractive when tanned. The meat from the breast or flipper is taken. The meat is very black and rich. We cook the meat like swiss steak or pot roast. Natives boil and roast the sea lion meat and also make a brined meat of the flipper.

The wind blows and blows in one direction for two or three days, and then it turns around and blows back the other way. There are still movies, but they are reruns now, and bingo, basketball, and volleyball to keep us busy after school and in the evenings. During February and March the village, which is all Russian Orthodox, observes Lent. During this time there are no movies or social activities. The days are getting sunnier now, but they do not seem warmer. It is cold, 15° to 30°, maybe not cold by Interior standards, but cold when the wind blows constantly from 15 to 75 miles per hour.

We are eager for mail, but often we go a long time between delivery because of the miserable weather.

three . . . two . . . we get up in the middle of the night and look out to see if she's anchored out there in the dark. There she is. Now, pray for a good landing and no bad north or northwest wind. If the two landings are no good, she may have to sit there for days.

It's almost like Christmas already with the boat here. Packages, mail, letters going out, and fresh produce.

The *Pribilof* goes between the islands for only 7 or 10 days if the weather is good. Just enough time for the boat to unload at both islands, and for us to get our Christmas cards out. The boat's departure isn't such a great letdown because Christmas is coming, and there is a lot to look forward to. Saint George is just as exciting and excited as New York at Christmas.

After all, we get two Christmases and two New Years here in the Pribilofs. Traditional Christmas and New Year's and then Russian Orthodox

Jacob Pletnikoff helps stretch fox pelts. Arctic foxes are still part of the subsistence catch on the islands.

Andrew Rukovishnikoff acts out his version of Santa in Regina Browne's fifth and sixth grade class production of *The Night Before Christmas.*

Julie Melovidov tacks up letters of the alphabet during a kindergarten class on Saint Paul.

Bill Browne boils *oosik,* the penis bone of the walrus. This photo was taken before the Marine Mammal Protection Act, which took effect in 1972, made it illegal for non-Natives to have unworked marine mammal parts.

All photos by Bill Browne

We look forward to seeing a boat — any boat. Coast Guard vessels occasionally come in and pick up mail. We sometimes see Russian or Japanese fishing and crab ships. Even if we don't see them, we know they are out there by the constant activity on the short wave radio. If there is ice in March, we will see the Coast Guard ice breakers around.

This is the time to do all the things you have been putting off all year. Splice that film, fix those slides, polish that ivory you found, mend, sew, hunt, and read, read, read.

The winter really seems over at Easter. Social activity starts again. The birds are coming back. The *gavaruuckin* (kittiwakes) are good to eat. The *chuuchkin* (least auklets) are back, and everyone is out for birds. The children go out in the early morning when the *chuuchkin* fly. They arm themselves with rocks and sticks. The *chuuchkin* come whirring off the hill in back of the village in tight formation and whish overhead toward the sea — very low. The boys near the beach throw their sticks and stones and usually get two or three

93

of them with one throw. One person can easily eat two or three *chuuchkin* at one sitting as they are very small, so the boys must bring home 20 or 30 to feed the folks and brothers and sisters.

We find some mussels and clams on the beach and cook them up in a good chowder to go with roasted *chuuchkin.*

After Easter we begin to watch for the first bull seals to come in on the beach and set up camp again. We also begin to look for the return of the *Pribilof* for summer. School is almost out. Kids and teachers are restless. High school students will be home soon. Everyone is anxious to see their big brothers and sisters. It is almost summer. Another year on Saint George.

. . . later years

We spent another seven years in the Pribilofs after our first teaching assignment at Saint George. Many things changed during the late 1960s and 1970s for these islands. The coming of age has produced that bittersweet Alaska phenomenon — one foot in traditional subsistence living and the other foot in the 21st century corporate jet age.

When we returned to the Pribilofs in 1968, we were lured to the less isolated island of Saint Paul. What a change — motor bikes roamed about the island at all hours, plane service once a week, 30 plus miles of scoria-graveled road, and long stretches of beach to comb.

Prior to the advent of three-wheelers, it was an unwritten law that all beachcombing be done on foot, so many hours were devoted to the ritual of combing. There were so many small Japanese and Russian glass balls that washed up, we became quite finicky, only picking up those balls that were unusual or of larger size. A real treasure was the very large (18 to 24 inches in diameter) glass float. Impatient combers paced in front of windows and radios, watching and waiting for a storm to subside to hit the beaches.

The routine of life on Saint Paul was very similar to that of Saint George: waiting for the plane or the M.V. *Pribilof,* the school schedule and activities, bells ringing in the cyclical patterns of the church holidays. Socially, religiously, and ethnically, the islands are similar. Many of our Saint George friends had moved to Saint Paul, and it was very easy for us to return and fit into everyday life.

Time changes all things, and people grow and change too. Saint George now has a runway and scheduled flights. The M.V. *Pribilof,* M.V. *Snowbird,* and M.V. *Aleut Packer,* operated by Aleut Alaska Shipping Company, a subsidiary of the Aleut Corporation, provide marine freight service to the islands every few months. Some students still migrate to Mount Edgecumbe near Sitka for school, but this too may change soon. Women still bake their marvelous *puruugax* (fish pie), *piiruushkan* (meat pastries), and bread. Men still hunt for sea lions along the cliffs, and children still chase *chuuchkin* in the spring.

Now many people own their own businesses on both islands. The Pribilovians run their own corporations, stores, and schools. With growth come some of the more dubious gifts of modern society — TV, telephones, drugs.

In 1978 we left the Pribilofs for the third time. We still keep in contact with friends and still talk of returning sometime. There's always a bit of surprise when people ask "How did you stand the isolation and the wind blowing all the time?" because when we think of the islands, it is rarely of the wind and never of the isolation. Our memories are of that first step off the plane, and the smell of the salt air, and the sound of the seals bleating on the beaches. We think of the ever-changing sea and sky colors, and the lush green of the grasses, precious flower miniatures, the berries, the beaches, and the neatly tucked village as you round the hill with the Orthodox church spire dominating the center. We were not isolated but surrounded by an active community life and good friends.

Vikenty Tetoff (left), Bill Browne, and Logan Tetoff try to work a beached dead walrus higher up the beach on Saint Paul Island.

As the Aleuts of the Pribilofs strive to wean themselves from the federal government's purse strings and build a solid, diversified economic foundation, they hope, too, to preserve their traditional Aleut way of life.

In a Russian Orthodox ceremony on Saint George, Father George Pletnikoff marries Dmitri Lestenkof and Vera Esmilka.

Traditional Living in a Modern Society

By Larry Merculieff

Some 1,000 tourists visit the Pribilofs each summer on organized tours. The visitors come to see the fur seals and birds. What is not readily visible to the average visitor is the life of the island's human inhabitants.

The Pribilof Aleut culture encompasses ancient knowledge and present-day economics. The villages of Saint Paul and Saint George are modern, with wood-frame homes in orderly rows, heated by modern furnaces and having all the conveniences provided by electricity. The villages have street lights and well maintained roads by Alaska village standards.

Within the modern village setting, many traditional and non-traditional aspects of Aleut life can be seen. The centers of Aleut life are the Russian Orthodox church, the extended family, communal activities, and children. Pribilof Aleuts have been devout Orthodox Christians for more than 150 years. The elegant Orthodox churches are located in the center of the villages, a symbol that they are the center of Aleut life. Religious holidays are strictly observed. On such holidays all recreation

Editor's note: Larry Merculieff, president (1982) of Tanadgusix Corporation, the Saint Paul village corporation established under the Alaska Native Claims Settlement Act, was born and reared on the Pribilofs and has served for many years as a leader of the Pribilof Aleuts. Here Larry describes some of the traditions that are interwoven into the contemporary lifestyle of his people.

Douglas W. Veltre

Far left—The Aleut people adopted Russian Orthodoxy when they came under the Czar's influence. Today the religion is still strong in the Pribilofs. Here Iliodor Philemonof, former president of Tanaq Corporation and a trained church leader, shows off the beautiful icons and adornments of the church at Saint George.

Left—Huddled against the wind, Larry Merculieff waits calmly for passing sea lions near Northeast Point on Saint Paul.

Nekita Melovidov's face shows the remains of a vigorous pie-eating contest during Fourth of July festivities on Saint Paul. Priscilla Stepetin (in red) and Melinda Mandregan (in blue) share in the good times at one of the celebration's favorite events.

Carla Emery

and hunting stops. Traditionally, Lent, culminating in Easter, is strictly observed for seven weeks. Church services are held every day the first week and the seventh week, called Holy Week. For the other five weeks services are held on Saturday and Sunday and twice during the week. Twice a year, the priest and the village choir visit each household to sing religious songs and to pray with the family. At such times, every household opens its door to symbolize its welcome.

After church services, on major holidays, it is traditional to invite one's extended family to a feast, usually at the home of the recognized family head. Aunts, uncles, cousins, brothers, sisters, and always their children come to these gatherings. Usually food served on these occasions consists of Aleut delicacies such as *puruugax* (fish pie), *alaadiks* (fried bread), and pies filled with mossberries picked during family outings in the fall. The conversation, sometimes in Aleut and sometimes in English, centers around hunting, when the grocery supply ship will arrive, and who is getting married. These gatherings are always a time to dote on children, a happy time to catch up on what is happening with the family and events in the village.

Village life focuses on the children. The grandparents' role is to spoil the children on their frequent visits between households. Children are given free reign in their access to the village and the homes. Parents are totally comfortable in sending their three-year-olds out to play anywhere they please in the village because they know everyone looks out for the little ones. If a child is playing where they shouldn't, someone inevitably takes time out from whatever they are doing to shoo them away. If a child is wanted at home, a call goes out over the C.B. to send the child home. Every household has a C.B. radio set to one community channel. Discipline of the children is firm but loving.

In the winter, main streets are blocked off so that children can go sledding with their sleds and saucers. During Christmas, the village purchases

Douglas W. Veltre

Simeon Melovidov (left) and Nekifer Kochutin, Jr. lock hands in a battle of strength during Saint Paul's Fourth of July festivities. Besides sealing, Fourth of July is the major summer event on the islands.

Craig A. Hansen

John R. Merculief (left), Stan Bippus, Douglas Melovidov, and Patty Bippus hang on tight while Matfey Fratis on a competing team looks on at the centipede race during Fourth of July festivities.

101

Innokenty Lestenkof, here explaining the techniques of using an Aleut spear, is one of a long line of skilled Aleut hunters. The Aleuts far surpassed the Russians in their ability to catch marine mammals, and for this reason the Russians forced them to hunt for meat and to fill the holds of Russian ships with furs.

Lael Morgan, Staff

gifts for every child. Santa arrives by four-engine prop plane on one of the twice weekly flights, and rides on the village fire truck in a parade throughout the community. On Christmas Eve, after the community Christmas program, Santa appears when the entire population sings "Here Comes Santa Claus."

In the winter individuals occupy themselves visiting neighbors for tea, playing basketball or volleyball, or playing bingo. The women attend community bingo games for fun and socializing. Women play a key role in communicating information in the villages during their social outings. These are times to exchange rumors, facts, and opinions. This Aleut grapevine efficiently transfers important information. If someone new comes to live in the village, someone dies, someone breaks up a romance, it is known throughout the entire village in a few hours. Consequently, it is impossible to make a mistake that breaks community tradition or values without the rest of the village learning of it in short order. In one sense, a person's private activities are public and are therefore tempered accordingly by peer group pressure. Aleut leaders are well aware that what is discussed over tea may change a crucial village decision.

In January the Pribilof people traditionally have *mus-kaa-raa-taax* and *us-xee-nok-thax*. For one week, in the evenings, individuals masquerade in blankets or sheets which completely cover them from head to toe. These *us-xee-nok-thax* go from house to house with a pot in hand, loudly stomping their feet. When the door to the house is opened, a member of the household places food or candy in the pot, and the masquerader leaves without a word. During this time, the Pribilof people gather once a night at the community hall to watch or dance with the *mus-kaa-raa-taax,* who are local individuals disguised in every imaginable form. Adults come dressed in mock diapers, as monsters, ballet dancers, or in anything their wild imaginations can create. Custom dictates having at least one monster at these gatherings to scare the children.

It is common to see village men with rifles and shotguns sitting patiently among the basalt boulders on the shoreline in winter and early spring waiting for ducks and sea lions to come by. A casual observer may see some of the cultural aspects of the hunt, practiced for generations, but only if he knows what to look for. The hunters are experts in the habits of the sea lion, a winter delicacy for the villagers. From childhood, Aleut hunters learn to closely observe nature. To successfully hunt sea lions, individuals must learn the animal's swimming patterns, and time their shots accordingly. Hunting sea lions calls for excellent marksmanship skills because the animals usually move quickly in and out of the high surf, 50 to 100 yards out, with only their small head showing. Hunters must know the tides and currents in the area to determine where a sea lion will come ashore if it sinks when shot. The hunter watches an unusually violent and foaming surf for glimpses of a flipper breaking the surface. Upon spotting the sea lion, the hunter swings a sea-dog — a piece of wood with sharp hooks attached to a long rope — in a wide circle and throws it beyond the animal, attempting to snag part of it on the hooks. Only the

Interest in halibut fishing starts at an early age on the Pribilofs. One fisherman's daily catch lies spread out at East Landing on Saint Paul.

Douglas W. Veltre

Workers prepare to hoist a *baidar* from the water at Zapadni Bay on Saint George to the back of a waiting truck. *Baidars*, which are used to lighter freight to and from large vessels offshore, are stored on land when not in use.

advantage of calm seas to fish for halibut. Generations of knowledge and experience come into play when an Aleut goes fishing in a 14-foot, outboard-powered aluminum skiff five to seven miles out in an unpredictable Bering Sea with only a hand compass for protection against frequent dense summer fog. The fishermen changed from old-Russian-style wooden boats to aluminum skiffs for ease in launching from concrete docks that lack launching aids. Standard gear for fishermen are thermos bottles of coffee, a compass, two handlines, herring or some other bait, life jackets, a hand-held C.B. radio, and two gaff hooks. The fishermen, always going in pairs for safety, traditionally fish halibut hotspots, each of which have names and are known only to the partners. Listening to an experienced fisherman teach a greenhorn is a lesson in nature and survival skills.

Notice the landmarks on shore. We always know our position in the beginning of a run so that we can come back to it if we hit a good spot. It's important too to know our position in case we hit fog. The compass can tell you which way is north or south, but it won't do one bit of good if you drift so far parallel to the island in a fog that you miss the island completely even with the right compass direction. If you're in ground fog at sea, use the sun to guide you in to land. When you go west, the sun is always on your left shoulder. Halibut bite best when the tide is changing to go south. You can feel if the halibut is not hooked good by how it fights. Never let the halibut get above water because as soon as it feels air, it will fight by the boat and you will lose the halibut.

These fishermen's skills have brought halibut fishing to the realm of art. The fisherman who catches the most halibut receives stature among his peers.

To preserve traditional ways, the Pribilof Island

experience of these hunters makes the retrieval look easy. Meat is distributed among the hunters according to who first shot the animal and to the cultural status of the hunters. If hunters with equal status shoot the animal, they know almost instinctively who shot it first. If one hunter had cultural rank, he usually takes the first shot.

Springtime is a season for hunting birds underneath the dark cliffs or stalking ducks resting in the small lakes on their northward migrations. A staple in the Aleut diet, murres are shot in large numbers on their flight to and from the cliff ledges. The types of ducks taken on the lakes depends strictly on opportunity; whatever is shot on the lakes is eaten.

Beginning in June, the city of Saint Paul prepares for the upcoming fur seal harvest. On Saint George, where there is a moratorium on fur seal harvesting, workers maintain federal facilities and assist the biologists who study the seals.

After a day's seal harvesting on Saint Paul and after 5:00 P.M. on Saint George, Aleut men take

Penny Rennick, Staff

Laurie Skelly

Students gather around Father Michael Lestenkof, Russian Orthodox priest on Saint Paul. Father Lestenkof encourages student participation in church activities, and during services the church is filled with young people from throughout the community.

Wearing signs urging the federal government to give islanders more time to prepare for the government's withdrawal from the Pribilof Island Program, students picket a meeting of island officials and government representatives on Saint Paul in late 1981. At the near end of the table on the left is Larry Merculieff, president of Tanadgusix Corporation, the Saint Paul village corporation. Walter Kirkness, head of National Marine Fisheries Service's Pribilof Island Program, sits with his back to the camera.

Both photos by Penny Rennick, Staff

School District has inaugurated a bicultural education program. Textbooks on Aleut history and culture, and Aleut language classes, acquaint younger Pribilovians with Aleut traditions. Community residents come to the school to teach traditional skills. At the same time the facilities, workshops, and library of the well-equipped school are open to the community. Older students do not have the advantages of this program because juniors and seniors are sent off island, to Anchorage, Palmer, or Mount Edgecumbe, for their final two years of education.

Students work actively to preserve their Aleut heritage. They have built a *barabara,* or sod home, on the school grounds. Students formed political parties, elected candidates, and picketed meetings of island leaders and government officials to urge the federal government to give the islanders more time to adjust to the government's phase-out of the Pribilof Island Program.

The Pribilofs are truly a place where one can observe how thousands of years of Aleut culture have adapted to the modern world. Pribilof Aleuts are no strangers to change, sometimes even drastic change. Even now the islanders are planning to sever their intricate and long-lasting ties to the seals. The United States government, which manages the fur seal harvest and is the major source of employment, is cutting its budget and intends to pull out the Pribilofs completely within the next few years. The Pribilof people are preparing to let go of 200 years of a special lifestyle to enter the world of fisheries and other economic opportunities. The Bering Sea may very well be the richest fishery in the world today. The location of the Pribilofs has been described as like the only aircraft carrier in the middle of a strategic war zone. The Pribilof Aleuts are carefully plotting the course of their vessel to ensure their survival. Aleuts have lived under the harshest of conditions in the most trying of circumstances for 10,000 years, and they have confidence in their abilities to survive in a new world of their own making.

The Saint George road crew lines up with some of the ancient government equipment they managed to keep going. Saint George Island has about 10 miles of scoria-covered road.

Top—Laurie Skelly talks with John Rukovishnikoff and Willard Krukoff, two of her students, during her language arts class. In addition to traditional subjects and a bicultural program, the school offers a variety of practical and life skill classes, newspaper and drama programs, and the latest in electronic instruction.

Above—Phillip Lekanof studies the scoreboard at the Saint George Elementary School. Because students in the higher grades are sent to Saint Paul, Saint George's enrollment is much smaller than that of its sister school.

Lael Morgan, Staff

Strangers always attract the curiosity of village children at Saint George. Here Gary Merculief and Shannon Merculief (no relation) pose for a visiting photographer in front of the fire station.

Survival for the 750 Aleuts of the Pribilofs will take ingenuity and a willingness to forego traditional reliance on the fur seals. Leaders of Saint Paul and Saint George have formed an interorganizational council to deal with major economic problems facing the islands: how to generate employment and income when the federal government pulls out of the sealing, how to pay for community services such as utilities, and how to support a marine shipping service to bring supplies to the islands.

Employment is the biggest problem. Without jobs young people leave to work on the mainland, and only the elderly, who survive on pensions, remain on the islands. The school district, city of Saint Paul and village of Saint George, the Indian Reorganization Act council, and the Public Health Service do provide some local employment. Tourism, which centers on Saint Paul but could be expanded to Saint George, means one full-time summer position and one part-time position on the islands. Tourists also generate substantial income during the summer for the King Eider Hotel and King Eider Restaurant on Saint Paul. Few tourists make it to Saint George, but for those who do, the National Marine Fisheries Service maintains the Company House with rooms for rent and cooking facilities. There is no restaurant on Saint George, but groceries are for sale at the village store and canteen. Tanaq Corporation leaders hope to expand tourism on Saint George by offering boat excursions to High Bluffs and some of the island's other spectacular bird cliffs.

The Future

Martha Krukoff has seen much change come to the Pribilofs over the decades. She recalls the harsh times of internment in Southeastern Alaska 40 years ago when pregnant women were left to fend for themselves with little or no medical care.

Tourism is one of the few non-governmental revenue sources in the Pribilof economy. About 1,000 visitors come to the islands each year on tours sponsored by Alaska Exploration Holidays and Cruises.

Lael Morgan, Staff

Penny Rennick, Staff

A fresh stock of groceries lines the shelves of the Saint George village store. Food is expensive — a box of Triscuits is $2.50 — on the islands whether ordered by mail and shipped in, or purchased from the local store.

Above—Saint Paul and Saint George leaders meet with State Senator Bob Mulcahy (center with solid blue shirt) at a planning session to consider the Pribilovians' options in light of government phase-out of the Pribilof Island Program. At far left is Larry Merculieff, president of the Saint Paul village corporation; third from right is Iliodor Philemonof, president of Saint George village corporation.

Right—Boxes of gravel wait to be unloaded from a barge at West Landing at Saint Paul. Empty boxes are used to package seal skins and blubber for shipment off the island.

Craig A. Hansen

Ric Robinson

Penny Rennick, Staff

Ric Robinson

The federal government currently subsidizes the costs of electricity and other utilities on the islands. On Saint Paul drinking water is available in the houses, but on Saint George villagers must fill containers from a tank in the lobby of the clinic. A phone system has been installed on Saint Paul where a $150 monthly bill for usage is not uncommon.

Although Aleut Alaska Shipping Company brings some marine transportation to the islands, without bulk fuel storage facilities, the Pribilofs will have a hard time attracting more marine shipping. The State of Alaska is funding expansion of the runway at Saint Paul to 6,500 feet, and plans are to bring in jets rather than the prop planes that have served the island in the past. Larger planes could mean more tourists and lower costs for shipping in food and supplies.

Lower freight rates would be a boon to the islands. Although the village store on Saint George operates in the black, the one on Saint Paul carries substantial debt. Because of high prices at the store, Saint Paul residents order their groceries through wholesalers in Anchorage. This drains the store's income and forces managers to also order merchandise by air freight because they cannot put together a big enough order to justify bringing in a barge. Air freight pushes up the price even more and makes it less likely that villagers would shop at the store.

Several other stores compete with the village store for the islanders' business. Anna and Terenty Philemonoff run the Burger Palace and gift shop in uptown, the new section of Saint Paul to the east of the main community. Anna and Steve Lekanof operate a curio shop in the basement of their home.

Terenty Merculief holds a model of a *baidar* he made using the same techniques his ancestors applied in making the real thing.

Tourists occasionally find their way to the curio shop for post cards, T-shirts, and Pribilof stationery. And Father Michael Lestenkof, Russian Orthodox priest on Saint Paul, oversees Lestenkof's Cafe which serves sandwiches and other short orders.

Tanadgusix and Tanaq corporations encourage their members to develop skills and crafts which might bring in additional income. Ludy Mandregan on Saint Paul teaches skin sewing when suitable fur seal pelts are available. The supply of pelts has diminished in recent years, which has curtailed skin sewing activities. A few women on Saint Paul make Aleutian grass baskets; Doris Krukoff still makes baskets in the Unalaska style.

On Saint George, Ariadna Lekanof helps out at the school and in her spare time makes seal throat baskets and pouches, reviving a skill of her grand-

115

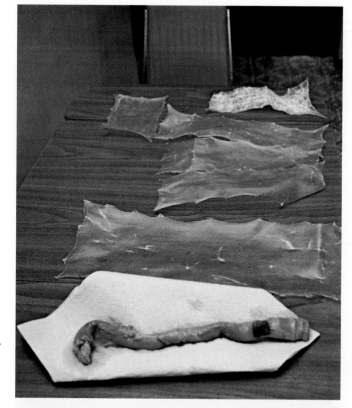

A moist seal throat and several dried, stretched throats waiting to be crinkled lie on the table of Ariadna and Peter Lekanof's home at Saint George. The largest throat is from a sea lion rather than a fur seal. Ariadna and her family fashion baskets and bags from the dried throats.

Ariadna used a piece of fur seal pelt and fur seal teeth to decorate this seal throat pouch.

All photos by Penny Rennick, Staff

parents and early-day Pribilof people. Her husband, Peter, and several of her children help prepare the seal throats. First the throats are soaked in water, then cleaned. The inner lining is then pulled from the throat, slit, and tacked to a board for stretching. The lining is left on the board to dry for a day or two. Next Ariadna or Peter or one of their eight children crumple and rub the lining, now stiff, by hand to create the crinkle design. After cutting a pattern from the crinkled lining, Ariadna uses a needle and embroidery thread to sew the basket pieces together. Taffeta is used to line the baskets or bags, and seal skin strips, mallard and gull feathers, and seal teeth decorate the outside.

To supplement their food supply, Ludy Mandregan and three or four other families on Saint Paul have livestock. Before World War II, livestock were common on the islands; the federal government maintained sheep and a dairy herd. But disruption of the war and the cost of transporting feed brought this fledgling agriculture to an end. Most of the animals now on the islands come from the schools' 4-H programs. Ludy has a goat, Lucy, and her kid, Filbert. Other families have geese and chickens.

On Saint George, Susie Merculief looks out her window to a fenced yard with chickens, ducks, geese, and a turkey. The turkey was slated for the Thanksgiving menu. The arctic foxes on Saint George are plentiful and not particularly afraid of humans. The foxes come sniffing around the pens, but stakes are driven several feet into the ground to prevent them from reaching the poultry. "Every time I look out my window, it's like looking at money in the bank," said Susie Merculief of her flock.

A few Pribilof families try gardening. On the south side of Tracy and Ludy Mandregan's home on Saint Paul onions, kale, potatoes, and lettuce grow in a box with a removable cover that functions like a greenhouse. Some have tried gardening at Zapadni Bay on the south side of Saint George but with no great success.

Left—On Saint George arctic foxes are common and not particularly afraid of humans. The animals sleep alongside houses and constantly explore any possible source of food around the village. This handsome fox with its white coat really stands out among the predominant blue color phase arctic foxes on the island.

Below—With government phase-out of the Pribilof Island Program, jobs and services usually supplied by the government will no longer be available to the Pribilof people. As their economy tightens, islanders turn more and more to poultry, livestock, gardening, and greater use of subsistence resources to supply needed food. This chicken scratches out a meager existence in a Saint Paul back yard.

Safe inside their pen, these geese keep a sharp eye on a hungry fox prowling outside their pen on Saint George.

*This page clockwise from right—***Andronik Kashevarof walks his geese past the cemetery on a small hill just behind Saint George village.**

At milking time Lucy, the goat, leads her kid, Filbert, and Ludy Mandregan into the back yard where Lucy will give enough milk to feed Filbert and the neighborhood cats.

A small, wily blue phase arctic fox peers from a tussock at High Bluffs on Saint George.

118

Craig A. Hansen

The Pribilofs have another resource, their reindeer, whose meat feeds the Pribilof people and whose hide is used in making crafts. Approximately 350 reindeer forage on Saint Paul, descendants of a herd originally brought to the islands in the early 1900s. About 100 animals are taken annually for subsistence on Saint Paul. In 1980, 30 reindeer were brought by boat from Unalaska to Saint George Island; 10 animals survived the trip and form the nucleus of a herd of 15 now on the island.

Petroleum development in the Bering Sea is not expected to generate much immediate income for the Pribilof people. Oil companies may look to the islands as a staging area for development in the Navarin and Saint George basins, but these activities are several years down the line.

All prospects for a solid economic future for the islands seem to center around the Bering Sea and its rich marine life. Tanadgusix Corporation has been experimenting with a halibut fishery, and a hair crab export program to Japan. The islanders have a history of subsistence fishing, but commercial catches have been beyond their grasp because the Pribilofs lack a harbor suitable for large vessels. Several agencies have studied ways to build a harbor for the islands, but all plans are costly and have drawbacks.

While waiting for harbor development, Tanadgusix Corporation set up a day-boat program with two small fishing boats that could be launched by hand. This gave prospective fishermen experience with small boats equipped with the latest in electronic gear and capable of fishing for several species. The corporation also established a 300-hour fisheries training course. Those who successfully complete the course will be eligible for corporation assistance in obtaining their own boats.

To promote Pribilof halibut, Tanadgusix arranged to fly fresh halibut during the legal season into Anchorage for sale to local restaurants and fish markets. They found, however, that transportation costs precluded profit. The islanders are now

Reindeer are one of the few land mammal resources on the Pribilofs. About 350 animals graze in Saint Paul's interior; a handful of reindeer forage on Saint George.

119

Both photos by A.D. Chandler

Max Lestenkof (top) and Anthony Philemonoff haul in a halibut as part of the fisheries development program in the Pribilofs. The first phase of efforts to develop a halibut fishery called for fish to be shipped fresh to markets in Anchorage, but transportation and other factors prevented this market from generating a profit. Plans now call for halibut to be frozen for shipment.

Pribilof fishermen collect a few hair crab from their pot. Islanders hope to develop a market for hair crab which abound in Pribilof waters.

Fishermen clean the F.V. *Anganta Qumax* and F.V. *Anganta Qaxchiiklu* after the halibut season. These two small boats are equipped with the latest in fishing gear and navigational instruments and serve as the nucleus of a small day-boat fleet for the Pribilofs. These boats are intended to give islanders experience catching a variety of species with modern fishing techniques and equipment in rough Bering Sea waters.

Craig A. Hansen

Penny Rennick, Staff

William Ermeloff (far right) testifies before the Commission on Wartime Relocation and Internment of Civilians at Saint Paul in late 1981. Commissioners visited the Pribilofs to hear firsthand accounts of the difficult conditions at the World War II internment camps on Admiralty Island in Southeastern Alaska.

turning their efforts to supplying halibut for freezing.

At the same time, Tanadgusix Corporation is searching for a market for the hair crab found near the islands. Japan will readily buy fresh crab, but transporting the delicate crustaceans across the Pacific has proven a problem. Current efforts call for the Pribilovians and Japanese to enter a joint venture for a floating processor to be stationed near the islands.

As time for the federal government's withdrawal from the islands nears, the Pribilof people are calling upon all their resources to search for a way to survive on the islands. As Larry Merculieff, who has guided much of this quest for economic viability, points out, "Whatever happens, the lifestyle in the Pribilofs will change drastically in the next five years." But the Pribilovians are used to surviving, and they are confident their skills in adaptation will bring them through this latest upheaval.

122

Ric Robinson

Just as this bird soars above lowering clouds and a restless Bering Sea, the Pribilof people are confident that they too can overcome hardships incurred with federal government withdrawal from the islands and move forward with a solid cultural and economic future.

123

Alaska Geographic. Back Issues

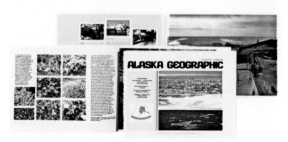

The North Slope, Vol. 1, No. 1. The charter issue of *ALASKA GEOGRAPHIC®* took a long, hard look at the North Slope and the then-new petroleum development at "the top of the world." *Out of print.*

One Man's Wilderness, Vol. 1, No. 2. The story of a dream shared by many, fulfilled by few: a man goes into the bush, builds a cabin and shares his incredible wilderness experience. Color photos. 116 pages, $9.95

Admiralty . . . Island in Contention, Vol. 1, No. 3. An intimate and multifaceted view of Admiralty: its geological and historical past, its present-day geography, wildlife and sparse human population. Color photos. 78 pages, $5.00

Fisheries of the North Pacific: History, Species, Gear & Processes, Vol. 1, No. 4. The title says it all. This volume is out of print, but the book, from which it was excerpted, is available in a revised, expanded large-format volume. 424 pages. $24.95.

The Alaska-Yukon Wild Flowers Guide, Vol. 2, No. 1. First Northland flower book with both large, color photos and detailed drawings of every species described. Features 160 species, common and scientific names and growing height. Vertical-format book edition now available. 218 pages, $10.95.

Richard Harrington's Yukon, Vol. 2, No. 2. The Canadian province with the colorful past *and* present. *Out of print.*

Prince William Sound, Vol. 2, No. 3. This volume explored the people and resources of the Sound. *Out of print.*

Yakutat: The Turbulent Crescent, Vol. 2, No. 4. History, geography, people — and the impact of the coming of the oil industry. *Out of print.*

Glacier Bay: Old Ice, New Land, Vol. 3, No. 1. The expansive wilderness of Southeastern Alaska's Glacier Bay National Monument (recently proclaimed a national park and preserve) unfolds in crisp text and color photographs. Records the flora and fauna of the area, its natural history, with hike and cruise information, plus a large-scale color map. 132 pages, $9.95

The Land: Eye of the Storm, Vol. 3, No. 2. The future of one of the earth's biggest pieces of real estate! *This volume is out of print,* but the latest on the Alaska lands controversy is detailed completely in Volume 8, Number 4.

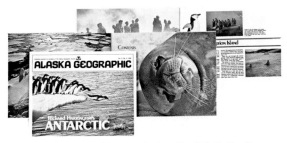

Richard Harrington's Antarctic, Vol. 3, No. 3. The Canadian photojournalist guides readers through remote and little understood regions of the Antarctic and Subantarctic. More than 200 color photos and a large fold-out map. 104 pages, $8.95

The Silver Years of the Alaska Canned Salmon Industry: An Album of Historical Photos, Vol. 3, No. 4. The grand and glorious past of the Alaska canned salmon industry. *Out of print.*

Alaska's Volcanoes: Northern Link in the Ring of Fire, Vol. 4, No. 1. Scientific overview supplemented with eyewitness accounts of Alaska's historic volcano eruptions. Includes color and black-and-white photos and a schematic description of the effects of plate movement upon volcanic activity. 88 pages. *Temporarily out of print.*

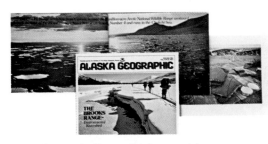

The Brooks Range: Environmental Watershed, Vol. 4, No. 2. An impressive work on a truly impressive piece of Alaska — The Brooks Range. *Out of print.*

Kodiak: Island of Change, Vol. 4, No. 3. Russians, wildlife, logging and even petroleum . . . an island where change is one of the few constants. *Out of print.*

Wilderness Proposals: Which Way for Alaska's Lands?, Vol. 4, No. 4. This volume gave yet another detailed analysis of the many Alaska lands questions. *Out of print.*

Cook Inlet Country, Vol. 5, No. 1. A visual tour of the region — its communities, big and small, and its countryside. Begins at the southern tip of the Kenai Peninsula, circles Turnagain Arm and Knik Arm for a close-up view of Anchorage, and visits the Matanuska and Susitna valleys and the wild, west side of the inlet. 230 color photos, separate map. 144 pages, $9.95

Southeast: Alaska's Panhandle, Vol. 5, No. 2. Explores Southeastern Alaska's maze of fjords and islands, mossy forests and glacier-draped mountains — from Dixon Entrance to Icy Bay, including all of the state's fabled Inside Passage. Along the way are profiles of every town, together with a look at the region's history, economy, people, attractions and future. Includes large fold-out map and seven area maps. 192 pages, $12.95

Bristol Bay Basin, Vol. 5, No. 3. Explores the land and the people of the region known to many as the commercial salmon-fishing capital of Alaska. Illustrated with contemporary color and historic black-and-white photos. Includes a large fold-out map of the region. 96 pages, $9.95.

Alaska Whales and Whaling, Vol. 5, No. 4. The wonders of whales in Alaska — their life cycles, travels and travails — are examined, with an authoritative history of commercial and subsistence whaling in the North. Includes a fold-out poster of 14 major whale species in Alaska in perspective, color photos and illustrations, with historical photos and line drawings. 144 pages, $12.95.

Yukon-Kuskokwim Delta, Vol. 6, No. 1. This volume explored the people and lifestyles of one of the most remote areas of the 49th state. *Out of print.*

The Aurora Borealis, Vol. 6, No. 2. The northern lights — in ancient times seen as a dreadful forecast of doom, in modern days an inspiration to countless poets. Here one of the world's leading experts — Dr. S.-I. Akasofu of the University of Alaska — explains in an easily understood manner, aided by many diagrams and spectacular color and black-and-white photos, what causes the aurora, how it works, how and why scientists are studying it today and its implications for our future. 96 pages, $7.95.

Alaska's Native People, Vol. 6, No. 3. In the largest edition to date — result of several years of research — the editors examine the varied worlds of the Inupiat Eskimo, Yup'ik Eskimo, Athabascan, Aleut, Tlingit, Haida and Tsimshian. Most photos are by Lael Morgan, *ALASKA*® magazine's roving editor, who since 1974 has been gathering impressions and images from virtually every Native village in Alaska. Included are sensitive, informative articles by Native writers, plus a large, four-color map detailing the Native villages and defining the language areas. 304 pages, $19.95.

The Stikine, Vol. 6, No 4. River route to three Canadian gold strikes in the 1800s, the Stikine is the largest and most navigable of several rivers that flow from northwestern Canada through Southeastern Alaska on their way to the sea. This edition explores 400 miles of Stikine wilderness, recounts the river's paddlewheel past and looks into the future, wondering if the Stikine will survive as one of the North's great free-flowing rivers. Illustrated with contemporary color photos and historic black-and-white; includes a large fold-out map. 96 pages, $9.95.

Alaska's Great Interior, Vol. 7, No. 1. Alaska's rich Interior country, west from the Alaska-Yukon Territory border and including the huge drainage between the Alaska Range and the Brooks Range, is covered thoroughly. Included are the region's people, communities, history, economy, wilderness areas and wildlife. Illustrated with contemporary color and black-and-white photos. Includes a large fold-out map. 128 pages, $9.95.

A Photographic Geography of Alaska, Vol. 7, No. 2. An overview of the entire state — a visual tour through the six regions of Alaska: Southeast, Southcentral/Gulf Coast, Alaska Peninsula and Aleutians, Bering Sea Coast, Arctic and Interior. Plus a handy appendix of valuable information — "Facts About Alaska." Approximately 160 color and black-and-white photos and 35 maps. 192 pages, $14.95.

Klondike Lost: A Decade of Photographs by Kinsey & Kinsey, Vol. 7, No. 4. An album of rare photographs and all-new text about the lost Klondike boom town of Grand Forks, second in size only to Dawson during the gold rush. Introduction by noted historian Pierre Berton: 138 pages, area maps and more than 100 historical photos, most never before published. $12.95.

Alaska Mammals, Vol. 8, No. 2. From tiny ground squirrels to the powerful polar bear, and from the tundra hare to the magnificent whales inhabiting Alaska's waters, this volume includes 80 species of mammals found in Alaska. Included are beautiful color photographs and personal accounts of wildlife encounters. *The* book on Alaska's mammals — from Southeast to the Arctic, and beyond! 184 pages, $12.95.

The Aleutians, Vol. 7, No. 3. The fog-shrouded Aleutians are many things — home of the Aleut, a tremendous wildlife spectacle, a major World War II battleground and now the heart of a thriving new commercial fishing industry. Roving editor Lael Morgan contributes most of the text; also included are contemporary color and black-and-white photographs, and a large fold-out map. 224 pages. $14.95.

Wrangell-Saint Elias, Vol. 8, No. 1. Mountains, including the continent's second- and fourth-highest peaks, dominate this international wilderness that sweeps from the Wrangell Mountains in Alaska to the southern Saint Elias range in Canada. The region draws backpackers, mountain climbers, and miners, and is home for a few hardy, year-round inhabitants. Illustrated with contemporary color and historical black-and-white photographs. Includes a large fold-out map. 144 pages, $9.95.

The Kotzebue Basin, Vol. 8, No. 3. Examines northwestern Alaska's thriving trading area of Kotzebue Sound and the Kobuk and Noatak river basins, lifelines of the region's Inupiat Eskimos, early explorers, and present-day, hardy residents. Contemporary color and historical black-and-white photographs illustrate varied cultures and numerous physical attractions of the area. 184 pages, $12.95.

Alaska National Interest Lands, Vol. 8, No. 4.
Following passage of the bill formalizing Alaska's
national interest land selections (d-2 lands),
longtime Alaskans Celia Hunter and Ginny Wood
review each selection, outlining location, size,
access, and briefly describing the region's special
attractions. Illustrated with contemporary color
photographs depicting as no other medium can the
grandeur of Alaska's national interest lands. 242
pages, $14.95.

Alaska's Glaciers, Vol. 9, No. 1. Examines
in-depth the massive rivers of ice, their
composition, exploration, present-day distribution
and scientific significance. Illustrated with many
contemporary color and historical black-and-white
photos, the text includes separate discussions of
more than a dozen glacial regions. 144 pages,
$9.95.

Sitka and Its Ocean/Island World, Vol. 9, No. 2.
From the elegant capital of Russian America to a
beautiful but modern port, Sitka, on Baranof
Island, has become a commercial and cultural
center for Southeastern Alaska. Pat Roppel,
longtime Southeast resident and expert on the
region's history, examines in detail the past and
present of Sitka, Baranof Island, and neighboring
Chichagof Island. Illustrated with contemporary
color and historical black-and-white photographs.
128 pages, $9.95.

NEXT ISSUE

The Alaska Minerals Industry, Vol. 9, No. 4.
Experts detail the geological processes and
resulting mineral and fossil fuel resources that are
now in the forefront of Alaska's economy.
Discussions of historical methods and the latest
techniques in present-day mining, submarine
deposits, taxes, regulations, and education
complete this overview of an important state
industry. Illustrated with historical
black-and-white and contemporary color
photographs. To members in August, 1982. Price
to be announced.

The Alaska Geographic Society

Box 4-EEE, Anchorage, AK 99509

The Alaska Geographic Society is a
nonprofit organization, and your $30 annual
membership brings you four big issues of
ALASKA GEOGRAPHIC®. Membership advantages
include substantial cost-savings on this award-
winning book-size publication and a guarantee
that you won't miss a single issue!
Each edition of *ALASKA GEOGRAPHIC®* is
devoted to a single subject, and that subject is
explored inside and out, with insightful text and
beautiful photos. Maps, illustrations, facts and
figures — they're all an integral part of what has
become one of the most well-respected
publications in the country . . . and abroad!